Non-Confrontational

SALES

A MODERN SALES GUIDE TO RAPIDLY IMPROVING IN-HOME SALES

BABE KILGORE

This book is dedicated to the hustlers. The workers. The go getters. The man or woman that creates something from nothing. This dedication goes out to the salesperson. Nothing in this world truly happens in business until somebody makes a sale. This book is dedicated to you. Thanks for making the world turn.

CONTENTS

Introduction

MODERN DIRECT SELLING

Hardcore direct selling is dead. The days of knocking on doors and being pushy and insistent about the sale are over. Your customers cannot stand it when you put them through that ordeal. They will not listen to you, and they definitely will not buy from you. Confrontational selling has become the biggest liability to sales teams today.

With the rise of digital technologies, connectedness, and social media, an entirely new code of ethics has climbed its way to prominence. It is called non-confrontational sales theory, and it is a scientific, measurable method of direct selling that is quickly replacing the outdated hard sell of yesterday. Best of all, it is easier and more rewarding to practice for everyone.

If you are staking your career or company on your ability to sell, then this book will be the best thing that has ever happened to you. The techniques in this book sell. And it does this by teaching you to reframe your opinions on your current sales theory while showing you how to effectively practice non-confrontational sales theory instead.

One-on-one selling is the most difficult form of sales to achieve, day in and day out. It takes a certain kind of dedicated and trained salesperson to set the pace and close multiple deals every week. The good news is that I have studied this method in multiple businesses and various industries, and it flat out works.

While the technicalities of the business are always different, the theory and practices remain the same. If you and your sales team are hell bent on learning how to close as many sales as possible, then you need to start practicing this modern method of direct sales.

As more businesses transition over, it is not just the company that benefits but the people on both sides. Customers love non-confrontational salespeople. These individuals are focused, organized, responsible, and ethically accountable. These are the men and women on the ground that are forming real relationships with people as they sell.

The Internet is only getting bigger. Social media has become a part of daily life. People have more choices than ever before. They know what a hard sell sounds like. Your customers will eventually choose to give their money to businesses that embrace non-confrontational sales theory because it is in line with what people expect.

Modern direct selling is here. It is time to get on board and accelerate your sales.

Let's begin.

Section I:

WARNING:
DO NOT CONFRONT!

Chapter 1

NON-CONFRONTATIONAL SALES THEORY

"Nobody wants to feel sold,
but everybody loves to buy "
ANONYMOUS

For the last fifty years direct-selling books have taught salespeople how to be fearless when facing the confrontational sale. Hard selling, characterized by advertising and sales practices that were aggressive and forceful, was how one-on-one sellers used to close sales on the job. It was a high-pressure technique that produced results.

Then came the Internet, social media, and a whole new age of connectedness, communication, and choice. The hard sell stopped working. Worse yet, the soft sell that took its place was inconsistent, unreliable, and difficult to teach to a room full of salespeople. Every direct seller was told, "Do not confront," and was left to muddle through the rest.

This Is How Non-Confrontational Sales Theory Works

The key to non-confrontational sales is *engagement*.

By learning how to effectively communicate with your customer using modern language techniques and the psychology of selling, you create engagement that allows you to influence a short-term sale by quickly gaining trust, credibility, and familiarity with your customers. Organization, preparedness, communication, and a deep understanding of your customers' needs are all required for this to work.

Correctly defined, non-confrontational sales theory is a set of principles and practices geared towards closing face-to-face sales using communication that reduces confrontation and thus creates high engagement so you can influence your customers' understanding of your product in a non-confrontational manner.

The goal with non-confrontational sales is to harness the power of human connection and influence together with ethical communication techniques to *engage* your customer and change their emotional state of mind. By doing this, you make them feel more strongly about buying your product than they do about *not* moving forward with you.

Everything in your sales process is transparent, and all the seller has to do is run through a sales script that they have practiced many times before while carefully employing the linguistic and psychological techniques that will help close the sale. Imagine how much better off you would be if you could close 80% of your sales on the same day because your buyer was engaged and understood your offering.

I want you to ask yourself a simple, straightforward question:

If people truly understood what it is you are selling, would they choose to buy?

The answer should always be yes. All that remains is how you choose to explain your product to your customer in order to make that happen. When you know the sale depends on *understanding*, your two greatest weapons are communication and emotion. If you can nail these two elements of non-confrontational sales, you will become formidable.

When you can learn to effectively show others how your product or service will add value in their life *and* they actually comprehend and fully understand what you are talking about, great things happen.

I dream of a world where direct sellers are greeted with warmth and anticipation at the door. A world in which face-to-face sales become a mutually-beneficial partnership and more than a lone individual with product to move knocking on random doors. Best of all, when communication and understanding are your central focus, you always leave a good impression behind.

The Death of "In-Your-Face" Sales: A Modern Retelling

I hate the term "sleazy salesman." It brings to mind the perennial image of the dirt bag car salesman in a yellow plaid suit with greasy hair, who would tell you the apocalypse will wipe out your family tomorrow if you do not buy the junk they want to sell you. What characterized these sellers back in the day was simple.

They were pushy, insistent, overly-confident, and aggressive, and they lied and used flowery language to push bad products onto unsuspecting buyers. These days, customers do not respond to pressure, and they strongly dislike the hard sell. Why? Because they know that the end goal for that salesperson is just money.

The last fifty years has conditioned buyers to be cautious of salespeople, because of their bad practices and lack of ethics.[1] Emotional walls immediately go up the moment a stranger steps into their home or when they answer a phone call from a telemarketer.

None of these experiences are perceived as fun, friendly, or even pleasant for the customer. No wonder the moment social media arrived, the world began to badmouth sales people at a rapid pace. I firmly agree with them. These hard sellers were only focused on the money they could make. They could not care less about the product, the customer, or if the customer needed the product. That simply was not the goal. The goal was the quick sale.

Salespeople have developed a specific image because of these unscrupulous types. They demand your trust, but they are not doing anything in your best interest. That is why they are forced to coerce, lie, and spin webs around the truth to make the sale. "Never trust a salesman" is a stereotype that every seller has to dispel as part of their job now.

That is why non-confrontational sales is so valuable—because it finally asks politely for trust, explains why the customer can and should trust the salesperson, and then proceeds to sell the customer something of great benefit. The difference is that the seller is helping the customer and being rewarded for it emotionally as well as financially.

Boiled down, confrontational sales says, "Buy this now," and stands there glaring at your customer in a yellow plaid suit.

Non-confrontational sales says, "Here is why you should buy this specific product from me," and then takes the time and techniques required to promote understanding.

---

1   Doomed for Failure: Hard Selling Is Dead, http://www.financialcopilot.com/doomed-for-failure-hard-selling-is-dead/

People want information. They just do not want to be forced to have it. Nobody wants to feel sold, but *everybody* loves to buy. Non-confrontational sales theory gives you the process and vehicle to do just that.

When the theory promotes improved relations between buyer and seller, great things happen. Hard selling was always a horribly flawed theory. Just because you can pressure people into buying things that they do not want does not mean that you should.

Sales companies that are not transparent and honest will quickly be revealed for what they are. The era of sales has evolved and taken that crucial next step. It is time to stop pretending; let's put the *direct* back into direct selling. It is time to invest in your own skills as a salesperson to move up the ranks and become a power seller.

Selling is transitioning into a more natural, friendly process, where both parties leave with something better than before. Customers want quality, honesty, and trust when they look to buy something important. It is the very least you can do for taking up their time. If you need to lie to sell your product, you need a new product.

Sales needs a new image, and together you and I are going to give it one with non-confrontational sales theory.

Chapter 2

YOUR EMOTIONAL BANK ACCOUNT

"A smart salesperson listens to emotions, not facts."

UNKNOWN

MEET DAN AND JOE

They have both been selling for three years using hard selling techniques. Dan has just joined a new company selling security systems. Joe has joined a competitor company selling the same system. Dan's company has embraced non-confrontational sales theory, while Joe's has stuck to the hard sale.

Throughout this book, you will see the differences between their direct selling techniques and why they are either effective or ineffective. To help you remember who is who in the examples, Dan has become a killer sales person and thus "Dan the man," while Joe, who is stuck in outdated confrontational sales, is "Slow Joe."

You are a walking advertisement. Everything you are, everything about you, down to the very last minute detail is transmitting data to the people around you. Whether you like it or not, you are like a walking, talking sales radar. In order to excel at non-confrontational sales theory, you will need to take a close look at...everything. Because everything influences your customer!

In this chapter, I am going to ease you into the fundamentals so that you can begin to make your shift from a hard selling grease ball to a trustworthy sales professional. It starts one person at a time, but once you have a team together running these plays, your reputation will reach higher levels than you could have imagined. Welcome to the world of direct selling as it was always meant to be.

Your Definite Purpose

Do you know what your definite purpose is? I regularly speak about it with my sales team because it is the very first thing that you need to get straight in your mind. I will reframe the question and let you think about it for a moment:

> *What is the ultimate goal or gain that you want to take away from your current job experience?*

I know it is a tough question. Most responses that I get center around family, college, and career. But this does not take it far enough. You have to understand your personal mission statement before you can get in sync with your sales style.

I want you to think about your definite life purpose and what your sales position means in relation to the progress you want to make. This will help you put your next few months into a financial context that will act as a motivating factor for the learning curve you are about to experience with non-confrontational sales theory.

Dan's reason for working in sales is that he wants to become a parent. Recently married, Dan and his wife want three kids over the next five years, and that means Dan needs to earn good money to start saving for schools, colleges, and other family expenses.

His definite purpose in life is to have a loving family and a good career and to be able to provide enough so that they can all live happily without financial stress. When Dan is asked about his definite purpose in sales this quarter, he says it is to sell 100 accounts.

Joe "wants to make money." He never thinks about his definite purpose and therefore is unable to set any short-term goals that are entrenched in his life plan.

Everyone in sales has a different definite purpose. It is essential to find yours so that you can add fuel to your sales rocket so that you cannot only succeed but thrive. And this is all based around a feeling that you want. You want to feel financially secure, and you want to feel successful.

Acknowledge that you are not in it for the money but for the feeling it will give you—the feeling of freedom.

Free Will vs. Determinism

There are two schools of thought that will govern your actions in the coming days. This may seem aggressive to you, but as a salesperson, you should already be familiar with convincing schools of thought and how there is no such thing as an absolute truth in sales. Philosophically speaking, there is either free will or determinism.

- **Free will**: The power of acting without the constraint of necessity or fate;[2] the ability to act at one's own discretion
- **Determinism**: For every event, including human action, there exists conditions that could cause no other event.[3]

The world is influenced heavily by both of these ideas. Have you ever thought about what our brains are truly made of? How does your mind, the control center of your entire body, actually work? Simple. It works through the collaboration of different types of chemicals within your brain matter.

Different things people see and experience will trigger different chemical reactions in their minds. This also means that different things that other people say or experience causes chemical reactions in your brain as well. Experience changes the chemically reactive nature of our brains—this is a fact.

Determinism says that because these chemicals control our feelings, this in turn controls our actions and reactions, and people do not really make choices—rather, they respond to what is influencing them based on the chemical signals in their brains.

Free will, on the other hand, is the opposite of this. Free will dictates that regardless of the chemical makeup and brain sensations that we may experience, we can still choose what we want to do. Think of an addict that is chemically dependent on a drug. They often say that they do not have a choice anymore; they need it. But what about recovering addicts?

These individuals found a way to withstand the drug through one or a combination of support groups, therapy sessions, feelings of remorse, religion, and anything else that can trigger enough chemical change (translated into motivation) that allows them to say "no" to their previous chemical dependence.

---

2   Free Will, http://plato.stanford.edu/entries/freewill/

3   Determinism, http://www.informationphilosopher.com/freedom/determinism.html

One chemical reaction can overpower the next if you know how to trigger it.

People can be influenced by both determinism and free will.

What this means to the salesperson is that through predictable behaviors, actions, and words, we can influence brain chemistry and promote specific feelings in our customers—like the feeling of desire. And the great news is that you can learn <u>what</u> to say, <u>how</u> to say it, and what <u>to do</u> while saying it—for the most chemically persuasive message possible.

The Powerful Psychology of Selling

There is powerful psychology involved in selling. To illustrate this point, think of the last time you bought a car. You showed up at the dealership wearing nicer clothes than you usually wear—because you want to seem like you earn more money than you do. The cars were all lined up on the showroom floor, detailed, with chrome finishes, and smelling like success.

You knew more or less what you wanted, but you were open to suggestion. The salesperson probably made their way over to you at that point, buttered you up, and achieved their goal. What was it? Did they whisk you away to the office to sign papers and talk about your five-year-long car payments? No! They got you inside the car.

The goal of a car salesperson is to get you in your desired vehicle so that you can *feel* how good it feels. The touch, the sound, the smell—everything fills you up and convinces you the time is right to buy. A test drive is highly effective because it nearly always ends on a positive note.

Once you got out of that car, the salesperson just had to reinforce the value you were getting from the car in order to close the sale. This was positive reinforcement for a feeling that was inspired the moment you experienced the thrill of driving a car that could belong to you.

These are psychological tactics that work on a similar level to non-confrontational sales theory. The psychology of selling is only about that one thing: *creating the right emotion!*

In fact, the less you talk about selling, sales, and the fact that you are a salesperson, the better. For example, people may not allow a security salesperson into their home, but they would allow a security inspection analyst in to check on their current alarm system and to see what new programs are compatible with their current system. So much of sales is about framing yourself, your product, and your company in a positive light. Again—people want information; they just do not want to feel pushed and sold in the process. When you position yourself in the right light, your customer chooses to engage with you, allowing you to share information to chemically change the way they feel about an idea or message. The more you can engage the customer, the more they will understand and buy from you.

You also need to be aware of your state of mind because it impacts the customer's state of mind. You need to go in with a plan that is poised to close the sale on a positive note, which means eliminating fear through planning, strategy, and knowledge. This is how you can prepare your mind to close deals.

The Emotional Bank Account

Perception is perhaps the most powerful influencing factor in face-to-face sales. As I mentioned earlier, you are constantly giving off a specific perception through key senses to everyone and everything around you, specifically through sight, sound, and touch:

- *Sight:* How people see you is important. It makes them feel a certain way about you. This can be positive or negative.
- *Sound:* What you say and, more importantly, how you say it is critical.

- *Touch:* How you touch and physically interact with people promotes either fear or trust.

Every vibe you send out into the world makes a difference because it bounces off people around you like echo-location technology. There are very few neutral vibes in the world, so people like you and your customer are constantly adjusting your perceptions for either good or bad, all the time. Big actions cause big shifts, and small items generally have a small impact.

Positive impact items that you have control over are what I call "deposits" because they go straight into the emotional bank account of everyone around you, adding trust, value, and truly a "positive emotional state." Negative perceptions that you release into the world are called "withdrawals" because they remove positive feelings and progress from the emotional bank account of those around you and leave a "negative emotional state."

Things generally have a higher impact than you would think at first because we oftentimes become immune to the negative items we "put out there." Think about those common everyday items that you use at work or at home. You may have some jewelry you wear on the weekends, but you would never wear the same bulky gold chain every day to work just because you like it. You and I know people who exhibit this kind of behavior. These people do not mean to leave a negative feeling and perception for the people around them. They just get used to this behavior, and it becomes "normal" for them. The key is being *aware* of it.

Imagine the scale in Figure 1 as your "Emotional Bank Account," or EBA as we like to call it. Every person has one for every relationship they have. It is not important how you perceive your customer relationship; what *their* emotional

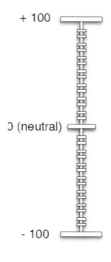

Figure 1

bank account does in reference to you is all that matters. Every positive perception you give off drives you up the scale and into a positive emotional state with your customer. Every negative perception you give off drives the feeling downward. And remember, it is the perception that matters, which is what they believe from their perspective!

Why are we making such a big deal about how people "feel" about you? Let me ask you a question. If you had to guess what percent of people buy on the following list of items, what would you say?

- Logic?
- Ego?
- Pride?
- Trust?
- Likeability?
- Value?
- Perception?

- Emotion?
- Other?

If you said anything other than 100% of buying decisions are based on emotion, then you were wrong. All those other items, and the countless others not on the list, simply change the way a person feels—emotionally—about you and the situation they are presented with. "Well, Babe...that doesn't make sense to me...." Think about it. If someone trusts you, they feel good about you. If the numbers make sense, this makes them feel good about it. If they want value, they feel good about it. Everything is emotion. Everything. All decisions. All agreements. All progress is based on how someone, some group, some company, "*feels*" about something else, and then they agree to either move forward or not. Harnessing those emotional feelings at every crossroad and interaction is the key to success. Master it, and you master decision making.

That is also why the good guy always wins in the long run—because they put out more positive vibes and influences than the bad guy. Remember that if during your sales process you end in the negative side of the Emotional Bank Account, you will never, ever make the sale. Plus, you can do terrible damage to your reputation by leaving the client with a bad feeling about you, your product, or your company.

If you end up in the positive side, meaning they feel "barely better about it," even if it is just a notch into the positive, you get the sale. This does not guarantee you keep the sale forever though. As we have all experienced, if you are one notch in the positive, the phone may ring the following morning with a customer on the other end that no longer wants to move forward. This happens because they were not high enough in the positive feeling that you deposited in their emotional bank account—and then they talked to a spouse, slept on it, had a neighbor say this or that, blah blah blah, and they cancelled their agreement with you. We have seen it a million times in sales. The higher you end on their emotional bank account, the better.

As they thought more about the costs, time, pressure, and fear of making a bad decision, by the morning, too many negatives had crushed the positive you left behind. Communication types will either turn the volume up or down on how quickly you can change the emotional bank account of your prospects.

This is because communication at the verbal, non-verbal, and meta-verbal level make up the perceptions that we send into the world as we sell. Get a handle on this, and you have a powerful weapon for closing sales.

The Heart of the Sale

As a salesperson, what is one of the first things you would do once you enter a home? Every salesperson has their routine. The goal of non-confrontational sales is to become so familiar with your processes that they move seamlessly from one step to the next.

That is why you should focus on exactly what you are going to say and how you are going to say it. Memorization is an essential part of this because it prepares you for the perfect pitch. As each step in the sales cycle arises, you need to be prepared for the next.

Once you get inside the house or the location where you discuss "the deal," you have truly made it through the hardest part. You now have the customer at a place where, as long as you do your job and communicate through non-confrontation sales theory, they are ready to engage and understand. You are their new non-confrontational friend, and they are ready to hear you out. Then it is a simple matter of delivering a friendly, engaging, and supportive pitch that takes them from fear to understanding and from negative sentiment to positive sentiment so that you can close.

I like to call this "the heart of the sale," and it is the most critical batch of techniques to get right in non-confrontational sales. Once you are in the heart of the sale, it is all up to the communication choices that you make.

In order to master the heart of the sale, you need to master these three types of non-confrontational sales communication. With control in these areas, you will quickly realize how basic memorization, presentation, and transparency add up to an exponential increase in sales.

In non-confrontational sales theory, there are three types of communication:

1. Verbal Communication: The science of choosing the right words so that you can absolutely nail the sales process and use the words that best influence the EBA

2. Non-Verbal Communication: Not what you say or how you say it but rather what you are doing while you say it

3. Meta-Verbal Communication: Understanding that how you say something is even more important than what you say

---

To recap, now you understand what non-confrontational sales theory is all about:

- Understand your definite purpose in life and in your sales career
- Understand that you are constantly giving off a perception to people, whether good or bad

- Understand that science proves that these perceptions alter the chemical makeup of your brain and thus deposit or withdraw feelings about you in your customer's emotional bank account
- Understand that small changes can create positive perspectives that allow you to influence those feelings to positively affect a person's perception about you
- Understand that every communication choice is critical
- Understand that the heart of the sale is where the magic happens—as long as you do your job and maintain a non-confrontational sales platform

Section II:

SELL IT LIKE IT IS: SALES COMMUNICA-TION

Chapter 3

VERBAL COMMUNICATION

"The two words 'information' and 'communication' are often used interchangeably, but they signify quite different things. Information is giving out; communication is getting through."

SYDNEY J. HARRIS

In section two, I will be detailing exactly how you can use verbal communication to win when you arrive at the heart of the sale. This will train you to sell it like it is while depositing positive vibes into your customer's emotional bank account. Remember that the more positive associations you can squeeze in there, the more likely you are to close the deal.

The first of the three core communication types is verbal communication. Surprisingly, this only accounts for a paltry 7% of the emotional bank account impact that you plan to have during your direct sale. Even though the influence is a small percentage, with every positive word you choose, you get closer to winning. A lot of small wins gets you a huge yes at the end of the sale. Here is how to do it.

Why What You Say Matters!

It is no surprise to hear that *what* you say makes a huge difference in your customer's perspective. It is true. Our brains are made up of soft tissue we call gray matter, but it is also made up of several other important things. Our ability to think, for example, comes directly from the chemical compositions in our brain.

Thoughts are actually just electro-chemical reactions firing off inside our 100 billion nerve cells, which are interconnected by trillions of synapses.[4] Each connection transmits one signal per second. Some connections can send 1,000 signals per second—which is how thoughts are formed.

These electro-chemicals create perceptions and feelings, which translate into thoughts and emotions. Every single perception—whether said, heard, smelled, seen, or felt—creates changes directly in the human brain. What does this mean, you ask? It means that all environmental or perceptual changes impact the chemical composition of your mind.

Translated, this means that everything you say or do, or do not say or do, matters because it makes a difference in how your prospect feels about you. The real impact or size of this difference is impossible to say as it varies from person to person. But small, positive changes can add up to make a huge difference!

Each time you choose a positive word that has a positive feel over one with negative connotations, you are adding a positive thought to your customer's emotional bank account. Every word counts because thousands of words are exchanged in our sales process, which can add up to an instant sale.

---

4   What Are Thoughts Made Of? http://engineering.mit.edu/ask/what-are-thoughts-made

The Science of Using the Right Words

In non-confrontational sales theory, you need to learn about the science of using the right words at the right time during your sales pitch. This means studying verbal communication and how it can impact your customer at any given time.

You need to understand the psychology of the sale and the impact that certain words have on your various customers. In the world of verbal communication, there are words in your chosen industry with positive associations and words with negative associations.

Understanding which is which will go a long way in helping you remove the wrong words from your sales scripts and will help you replace them with high-impact positive association words. A strong sales script with the right words will work miracles.

- If you only just made it through the door to your customer's home and you can sense a lot of apprehension and skepticism from your customer, a positive sales script worded the right way can offset their negative presumptions about your pitch. As you add positive associations through an intentional and precisely worded sales script, you can literally watch the behavioral changes being physically displayed as the mind of your customer gets put at ease.

- With enough positive associations in your customer's emotional bank account, the sale will not fall through. That is because when you leave them high into the positive of the EBA and with a good feeling about their decision, they will go through with the sale in every case.

- This also makes testing your sales scripts easier because you can review your success rate at each step of the sale and improve it as needed. If you lose the sale at a specific location, it may be because your script does not invoke enough strong positive sentiment in your customer at that time and point in the sale. You will then need to rewrite it to offset this.

Dan focuses on learning all about verbal communication and how it can influence a sale. He creates and tests his scripts, perfecting them until he achieves a high sales conversion rate.

Joe continues to sell by "winging it," which keeps his sales inconsistent. He has no way of tracking or refining his process, so he is never able to target a conversion rate or predict his sales progress.

Choosing Your Words Wisely: Vocabulary

Vocabulary is incredibly important in non-confrontational sales theory because it has the ability to shape a sale quickly. It is so important, in fact, that I insist on creating scripts and memorizing them for all of the sales teams I have trained over the years.

The goal is to target pull words and evict push words. Pull words are gentle and easy in nature—like "It makes a lot of sense when…" or "Based on my experience, customers have found that…." Push words are confrontational—like "You really *need* to look into…" or "You *must* understand that…."

You want to draw the customer into the sale by positively influencing them, so every little word counts. Your prospects are going to make decisions based on what they feel when you are sitting directly in front of them.

It is daunting to think about, but once you become good at this skill, it will feel like second nature. People have feelings according to what they see and hear. Your word choices are important because they can strike on specific emotions within your customer base.

Some common words to illustrate the difference might be as follows:

➤ Contract	✓ Agreement
➤ Paperwork	✓ Forms
➤ Cost, Payment, or Pay	✓ Investment
➤ Sales Presentation	✓ Analysis & Recommendations
➤ Sign	✓ Authorize, Approve
➤ Products	✓ Supplements

As you can see from this list, the words on the left drive negative connotations, while the words on the right are far more friendly and inspire positive sentiment. The words on the left withdraw positive influence from the emotional bank account; the words on the right deposit positive emotions into the emotional bank account. Simple!

This short list is just a small example. You will find these differences in every part of your sale and in all communication. The actual list that can be made is truly endless. You need to take the time to go through every single word from beginning to end and replace the negative words (or "less positive" words) with the best and highest positive emotional feeling replacement.

Here is an example from our two home security salesmen, Dan and Joe.

Dan: *Once your family is protected with your life protection system up and running, I was wondering if you knew anyone else that would be open to the friends and family promotion?*

Joe: *Once the sale is closed and your security system is working, I have more door knocking to do—do you have any neighbors' names I can follow up on and sell to as well?*

Dan says exactly the same thing as Joe just using non-confrontational language that keeps his customer in a relaxed, friendly, and positive frame of mind. He not only closes the sale but he gets referrals every time. The same cannot be said for Joe, who uses "sales speak," which is confrontational and sets his customers on edge. He loses the sale.

Focusing on Speech & Organization

The key to becoming a master verbal communicator is to put in the time and analysis required to refine the way that you speak to your customers. This means creating sales scripts that work and testing them in the open market. Have you ever written your entire sales script out from start to finish? If not, do not be lazy! Do it!

It will require a lot of organization on your part, and you will have to become so familiar with your product, your company, and yourself that you instinctively begin to avoid negative influence words. It takes some practice, but I can assure you—it is worth the effort in every way.

While verbal communication only counts for the smallest possible percentage of the psychological aspect of your sale, it is a critical function. When you couple the right word choices with the right non-verbal communication and meta-verbal communication (covered in the next chapters), it becomes exponentially more powerful.

Here is another simple example demonstrating the powerful effects of the right verbal communication:

> Dan: *Zoe and Peter's rooms also need to be covered with the new wireless technology to prevent an intruder from getting inside your home. The command center will notify you immediately if the life protection system or the smoke communicator is triggered.*
>
> Joe: *The kids' rooms should be covered to prevent the burglar from getting inside the house. The monitoring station will let you know if the security system or smoke alarm goes off.*

When you analyze these two scripts, you can see that Dan's is warm and personal, feels thoughtful, and is careful not to influence the customer negatively in any way. By using words like "home" instead of "house" and using the children's names instead of "kids," he successfully creates an emotionally personal touch and feeling of care in his presentation.

Dan may have spent several demos refining his script until it naturally has a high conversion rate. In the meantime, Joe is oblivious to the fact that he is reinforcing the idea that he is an outsider coming into his customer's house to make a sale. Not using the customer's children's names, for example, is distancing him from his prospects on a social level.

You need to focus on speech and organizing your scripts in a way that can be measured and improved upon over time. This is only done when you have a specific script that you use every time, and you can track where it breaks down and where it is successful.

Dan: *When your technician shows you the functionality of the home automation and security system, you'll see the value and benefits right away. I'm going to outline it for you right now so you can see why it makes so much sense to everybody I have talked to.*

Joe: *When you buy our security system, the costs are straightforward. Here is a list of the various costs involved with the service and the details attached to the sale.*

Cost vs. Value

The next two things I want to speak about are cost and value. Let's do a little exercise with Dan and Joe, our salesmen. Dan is going to address a customer using specific words, and Joe will too. Take note of how each salesman makes you feel:

You may have noticed that the two salesmen in our example are saying the same thing. Only for some reason, you feel more inclined to trust and buy from Dan than you do Joe. The reason for this is simple—Dan is aware of his verbal output and how it will impact your emotional bank account.

By using the term "value," Dan conjures images of savings, lifestyle improvements, ego, happiness, the avoidance of problems, the absence of pressure, no pain, feeling trendy, success, pride, and keeping up with the Joneses in the mind of his customer. Dan knows that this will instantly cause a positive chemical reaction in the brain.

Joe, on the other hand, has no idea that he is actively withdrawing from his customer's emotional bank account. Due to years of conditioning, the word "cost" is a trigger word that inspires feelings of losing money, losing time, losing energy, making the wrong decision, pain, threats, fear, and something they will never get back again.

Dan is moving to end the sale on a positive note by continually adding positive associations into the customer to put them at ease and to inspire the right feelings. Joe is tanking his sale by being ignorant of the many negative associations he has placed in his customer's mind, which have reminded him repeatedly that Joe is there to sell something.

Avoiding Misspeaking

When you first begin to practice non-confrontational verbal communication, you will mess up a lot. That is completely normal. The goal is to be aware of the words that you use so that you can be certain that by the end of the pitch, the customer has had enough successful positive associations to seal the deal.

This means that you may seesaw back and forth between negative language and positive language for a while. To limit this and eventually completely eliminate it from your sales pitch, you need to write a script for yourself and memorize it.

When you understand your sales process and have gained some experience by performing several demos at customers' homes, you will be better oriented on how to assemble scripts for every scenario along with having a natural affinity for positive words.

I insist that all of my sales staff memorize their scripts so that the impact of verbal communication is instant. The great thing about it is that if you mess up, you can simply start over again—adding to the positive influences by reverting back to your sales script. This happens a lot to new salespeople that are asked unscripted questions by customers.

Dan: *Here is the agreement for you to authorize.*

Customer: *Does this include all the payment terms and legal jargon we need to cover?*

Dan: *The costs are covered in detail, yes. Once your family is protected, your easy pay program for the discounted full service monitoring will begin.*

It should be a goal of yours to avoid misspeaking wherever possible by creating go-to scripts and memorizing them. Remember that you are trying to build a relationship with your customer, so in the beginning, it helps to be able to shift from a script to natural speech and back again. It saved my bacon more times than I care to admit in the beginning.

In the above conversation, Dan slips up and mimics some of the customer's negative sentiment by using the word "cost." He quickly makes up for it, however, by reasserting the family protection and the payment terms, which he describes as "easy pay" (or whatever term your company uses) to ease the customer's mind. The customer knows what he is talking about and continues with the sale in a positive frame of mind.

Improving Your Verbal Sales Communication

An ambitious, non-confrontational salesperson uses his sales script as a benchmark for results that they will record and analyze at the end of every week or month. Getting feedback from other team members or industry specialists and refining this script is key to improving sales conversion ratios.

A tested sales script with non-confrontational language should be able to close the vast majority of your sales. Once you have nailed your industry top sales closing targets, you have optimized your lead conversion system, and this script becomes a key tool for you to use in the prediction of future sales.

I never stop working on my verbal sales scripts, because I believe there are always better ways to sell with words. Tweaking a phrase or a word group here or there can sometimes have amazing results, but it does depend on the neighborhood you are targeting.

Dan, for example, might develop two main scripts—one for the short, quick sale if they feel like the customer is ready to close the deal early on and one for a difficult customer that needs to understand every last detail before the close can be initiated.

In three years of selling home security systems with non-confrontational sales theory and verbal memorization techniques, Dan is the team leader directing 60 team members with a tested sales script that has a 78% conversion rate.

In three years of selling home security systems with confrontational sales, Joe is still a team member struggling to make commissions every month.

The difference is the optimization of time, energy, and psychology in sales for advancement.

What does script improvement mean to you as a salesperson? More sales over time. Plus, if you create a script that works like a charm, you can build your own sales team and use this script as a working model, which will accelerate the entire team's sales results. All it takes is a bit of tracking during the week and some refinement on your part.

Start with a base script, and begin to develop a knack for memorizing them. This will serve you well on your non-confrontational sales journey. Remember, you are always the biggest asset that drives the close of any sale. Investing in your ability to write, memorize, and test scripts will advance your career.

Chapter 4

NON-VERBAL COMMUNICATION

"Pretend that every single person you meet has a sign around his or her neck that says, 'Make me feel important.' Not only will you succeed in sales, you will succeed in life."

MARY KAY ASH

The second part of perfecting your "sell it like it is" process involves learning how to work with non-verbal communication. Now that you understand that what you choose to say is important, you also need to realize that verbal communication is only the beginning. More critical to the emotional process of closing a sale are the non-verbal cues you offer your customers.

That means *purposefully* choosing what you are doing during the sales pitch. Things like body language, special zones, and body positioning count for a surprisingly large percentage of human communication, which directly impacts sales. In this chapter, you will discover several non-verbal methods of optimizing and priming your non-verbal communication skills.

The 38% Surprise

With verbal communication netting only a 7% influence on the emotional impact scale, it comes as a surprise to most new non-confrontational sales people that non-verbal communication is significantly more important than they may have previously thought. Thirty-eight percent of your impact on your customer's emotional bank account is coming from your physical communication.

Think about that number for a moment, and let it sink in. Your body and what it is telling your customers during the entire sales process is either working for you or against you. For many direct sellers, this is a terrifying thought as they cannot ever remember consciously using physical communication as a sales weapon.

Defined, non-verbal communication is *what you are physically doing while you interact with people whether you are using your mouth to speak or not.*[5]

As a salesperson, you are a human antenna that transmits data to those around you at all times. Learning how to communicate without words is a key skill that you should nurture. It includes learning how to deliberately use facial expressions, eyes, types of physical touch, dress, posture, and spatial distance to influence the emotions of the people around you.

---

5   Kendra Cherry, Types of Nonverbal Communication, http://psychology.about.com/od/nonverbalcommunication/a/nonverbaltypes.htm

Dan has been called in for additional training on his non-verbal communication skills. The organization wants to ensure that Dan understands non-verbal communication can never be turned off and that even silence says something during a pitch.

Dan is excited to learn what kind of messages he has been sending to his clients and how he can reshape these to be more in line with his sales goals.

Your Spatial Zones

Space matters. People do not tend to notice it until it is invaded or compromised by other people, but understanding how human beings respond to space can be a powerful influencer during your sales process. Like you, your customers have a comfort zone.

The last thing that you want is for someone to talk to you six inches from your face. Most people do not enjoy this with individuals they know well. With a total stranger—someone that is trying to sell them something, no less—this becomes intolerable. The first rule of your new client introduction is to give them lots of space. This space, which is critical during the initial interactions, brings down mental barriers so they do not feel threatened by you, allowing them to engage instead.

This spatial awareness starts from the second you knock on their door. By standing **six to ten feet away from the door** while committing to a slow approach during the introduction and presentation, you create a "safe zone" that puts the customer at ease.

Look at this example with our two salesmen:

Dan stands sideways (perpendicular), six to ten feet away from the door, as he has been trained to do. He knocks then retreats to the allotted space. When the customer looks to see who it is, they see a man some distance away, standing casually while waiting for a response. The space between them lowers the customer's guard, and the customer is free to investigate further.

Joe walks squarely up to the customer's door and raps on it with confidence. He stands directly in front of the door, facing directly forward. When the customer looks to see who it is, they see a man directly outside, and "forceful entry" is already emotionally implied. The lack of space inspires a negative emotional reaction, and some people choose to not open the door.

By the time Dan is qualifying the sale, his knowledge of non-verbal communication has allowed him entry into the home. He has become physically comfortable with the customer, chatting from a non-invasive distance at the table. Once trust is established, Dan may even move closer to the client if the signals are there.

At all times he considers if his client is comfortable with his physical distance. Spatial distance concerns are known as proxemics, and they are based on social norms, situational factors, personality characteristics, cultural expectations, and familiarity. The key is to be aware of it.

Body Positioning & Gestures

The second non-verbal cue to work on involves body positioning and gestures. It is important that you focus heavily on your physical movements and positioning as these will impact how your customer feels about you and what you have to say.

Body positioning and gesturing work hand in hand with spatial distance. Dan, for example, chose to stand sideways so that he would look smaller and less threatening to his customer as they approach the doored. At all times, your body needs to be relaxed and non-confrontational for your verbal and non-verbal communication to coincide.

1	Waving *(creates attention)*	7	Pointing *(attention, used to re-engage)*
2	Expressive hand display *(engagement and increased emotion on specific topic)*	8	Hands on hips *(creates power and helps confirm trust in your statements)*
3	Legs crossed *(relaxed)*	9	Arms crossed *(thinking, deciding, or feeling closed off)*
4	Standing vs. sitting *(standing = interaction and more confrontation, sitting = relaxed and conversational)*	10	Where you are looking *(focus, attention, or trust)*
5	Looking at your watch *(time rushed, wanting to be somewhere else)*	11	Rubbing your cheek *(deciding, thinking, unclear on a topic)*
6	Drumming fingers *(antsy, feeling pressed for time)*	12	Stroking chin *(thinking positively, leaning towards an agreement)*

Work on your deliberate movements (and what they mean), and practice using them during your sales process. Lawyers use them in court scenarios to sway jury opinion, so there is real power here! Here is a chart that you can use to focus on *deliberate* movement usage. How can you use the following to help create or keep engagement while staying non-confrontational?

*Key tip: For non-confrontational sales matters, *all* movements are done much slower than feels natural. This puts the customer at ease and keeps the conversation friendly and relaxed.

Posture is also something to consider as people are generally wary of strangers who enter their homes and act like they live there. Slouching, leaning, tapping, and getting too comfortable in your customer's home will send up a red flag for them. Get rid of those negative habits, and train yourself to sit upright, be alert, and be respectful of where you are.

On the other hand, too stiff a posture equals a salesperson who is "all business." Sit with the posture you would have if you were grabbing lunch in a public location with a friend you have known for 10 years. Relaxed but attentive.

Here is an identical verbal scenario that has a positive outcome for Dan and a negative outcome for Joe based on nothing but their body positioning and gestures.

Dan: *When your technician shows you the functionality of the home automation and security system, you'll see the value and benefits right away. I'm going to outline it for you right now so you can see why it makes so much sense to everybody I have talked to.*

Body position: Sitting neatly next to the client with direct, friendly eye contact, he has slow, non-confrontational body movements and is careful to focus the right amount of eye contact and gesturing attention on the document he is holding.

Joe: *When you choose to adopt our security system, the value you receive in return is huge. I'm going to outline it for you, and you will see the exceptional value here.*

Body position: Sitting directly across from the client, almost uncomfortably close, and leaning over to physically intimidate client, Joe looks at his watch twice during this sentence and has the agreement and pen in hand, which applies subconscious pressure for the customer to commit too early.

Results:

- The customer feels inspired and relaxed by Dan.

- The customer feels like Joe is rude/hostile and in a rush to make the sale.

Reading Customer Non-Verbal Cues

Just as important as being fully aware of your own personal non-verbal cues, you also need to learn to respond to your customer's non-verbal cues, or NVCs for short. Understanding what your customer is trying to say as you are talking to them can be the difference between a closed deal and a lost sale.

People cannot help but give us constant feedback on how they feel about things. All you have to do is train yourself to notice the subtle differences. Here is a list of body positions and gestures and the emotions they tend to emit.

	GESTURE	MOOD
1	Folded arms	Defensive
2	Rubbing their chin	Considering, thinking
3	Looking away from you or past you	Analyzing words
4	Staring at you as you are showing them things	Analyzing trust
5	Leaning back in their chair	Decision is made in the customer's mind
6	Sitting forward in their chair	Eager, listening
7	Cross legged, rocking their feet	Boredom
8	Increased blinking	Nerves and stress
9	Nose scratching	Disbelief and mistrust
10	Closing the eyes	Overstimulation of audio/visual
11	Raised eyebrows	Curiosity or interest
12	Leaning	Towards = like, away from = dislike
13	Fidgeting	Increasing discomfort
14	Shoulder shrug	Confusion, unclear
15	Partial arm cross	Lack of self-confidence
16	Finger drumming	Impatience
17	Ear pulling	Indecision
18	Nodding	Agreement
19	Sitting with legs apart	Relaxed
20	Hands in pocket	Disbelief, defensive

As Dan learns to read his customer's NVC, he will be able to make subtle verbal and non-verbal changes to his pitch, which will increase the likelihood that he will walk away with a sale. In the meantime, Joe—with his forceful method of selling—has no idea how inconsiderate, unwelcome, and rude his imposing body language makes him, and he is totally unaware of the customer's body language and thus cannot adapt his presentation accordingly.

The difference rests in the opposing sales methodologies. You need to look out for any of these obvious signs and adjust your behavior accordingly to keep the sale on track. The good news is that with this feedback, you can save a dying pitch.

Mirroring Your Customer

A powerful form of physical communication comes in the form of mirroring. This is an important part of keeping your customer involved and comfortable with you while you are at their door and beyond. As an initial strategy to put them at ease, I have seen mirroring get more salespeople through the door than any other method. But it is not the same old mirroring techniques your grandpa taught.

Everyone in the world has a comfort zone—you know that. Older methods of sales training have taught that you should copy and "mirror" the customer's behavior. That method is outdated. In non-confrontational sales, you always want to pull the customer into a non-confrontational and relaxed state of mind so you can create total engagement. If they are loud, stay relaxed and calm, and they will start to calm their voice and engage into the conversation.

In the beginning of this process, you may find yourself fighting against this strategy—because there are so many different attitudes that you will inevitably come across. Do your best to get your customer to mirror your relaxed motions, tone of voice, and calm nature until they fall in sync with you.

When you use body language effectively, it will set the tone for the rest of your sale. If you see that your customer needs to be calmer, for example, exaggerate slow gestures with a soft, calming tone of voice, and speak slowly. This is especially effective towards the close of your sale, when your customer is making the final decision to buy.

Mr. Green is leaning back in his chair, looking around and fidgeting. What does this mean for the salesperson that is trying to close the deal?

Dan would wait until Mr. Green was leaning forward, giving him positive signals before initiating the closing transition process. If his body language was not aligned with the next step in his pitch, he would need more positive language to get Mr. Green there. When it is there, he is confident and non-confrontational with a short and sweet close matched with non-verbal cues.

Dan: *Just authorize here.* (pointing to the authorization location)

Joe jumps in as soon as he finishes his parrot-style hard sell. Mr. Green turns it down.

Joe: *Just sign on the dotted line, Mr. Green, and I will call in the order to get your payment processed.*

Getting Your Customer Involved

Non-verbal communication is incredibly critical because it speaks to our basic instincts as human beings. Aside from communicating things that are quite separate from what you are saying, non-verbal communication can also enhance what you are actually saying—resulting in a more attractive, focused pitch.

The better you become at getting your customer to focus on what you are talking about, the more sense it will make to them. If it makes sense to your customer, then they will take the leap and want your product or service. Keeping the customer involved should be a priority throughout the entire sale.

Dan understands that when conveying emotion, if body language, tone of voice, and words disagree, then body language and tone of voice will be believed more than words. The effects are amplified!

Joe does not understand this and therefore has no idea why his customers do not respond to him when he says, "I'm delighted to meet you." In reality, it is because his body language betrays him as pushy, one-track minded, and insincere.

During your approach, have your customer get physically, emotionally, and imaginatively involved in the process. Get them to visualize concepts, hand them materials they can hold or see as you speak, and make it a real experience for them.

If you have to conduct a walkthrough in your industry, have the prospect with you to physically inspect everything, and be very expressive—this can help you recap things at your close. If your customer has been involved and focused the entire time, they will remember it when you deliver your final closing.

Another example of this is to allow your customer to use

your product on their own. As you talk them through it, show them how beneficial it is. When possible, have them physically hold and touch the product. Show them where the item(s) would be placed and how this is going to benefit their home and family. They need to physically see it to help them visualize it. If you can get them to imagine your product in their homes, along with all of the benefits they will receive because of it, they are much more likely to buy.

Eye Contact

Let's talk about eye contact and facial expressions—two elements that can and will sink your pitch if you let them. Eye contact is something all salespeople do, but there is always confusion over what the correct practices are for a non-threatening approach.

Appropriate eye contact should be maintained with your customer 50% of the time while you speak and 70% of the time while you listen.[6] This will communicate the ideal levels of interest and confidence to your customer. Eye contact must be made as you meet your customer, for four to five seconds. Allow your gaze to relax thereafter.

Always be aware of what you are looking at. If you do not meet their eyes again soon, they will feel that you have become disinterested, and negative withdrawals to their EBA might happen. Practice is really the only thing that will help you with eye contact.

Facial expressions are equally as important as eye contact when you are addressing your customer. You must present yourself as a relaxed, confident individual who knows what you are there to do and how to do it well. That means learning to

---

6   Jodi Schulz, Eye Contact: Don't Make These Mistakes, http://msue.anr.msu.edu/news/eye_contact_dont_make_these_mistakes

control your moods when you are with your customer doing a pitch.

The moment you enter a prospect's home, it is up to you to leave your own personal problems at the door. From that moment on, your facial expressions better be in line with what you are saying, or your customer will pick up on mixed signals and may become confused. Emotions like surprise, shame, anger, focus, happiness, fear, and boredom all reflect on the human face. An example of this would be moving to close the sale unconfidently with your eyebrows raised and shrugged shoulders, which obviously equals zero confidence.

Joe delivers a moving speech to his customer but fails to close the sale. When he probes into the reason why, Joe discovers that his customers kept seeing "exhaustion" on his face due to his extra-long hours. They interpreted this exhaustion as an overwhelmingly negative sign that they were not to trust Joe. Because of his non-verbal cues of exhaustion and his personal problems, the customers could sense the ultimate "sale killer" that reeks of the struggling old school confrontational sales rep. We call it "commission breath."

Dan, with his knowledge on facial expressions and eye contact, delivers a speech that is confident and closes the deal. He may also be exhausted, but thanks to his training and success, he is now mindful of coming across this way to his clients, who do not respond well to overworked and unconfident people.

Learn to study your customer's expressions for feedback, and practice arranging your face in ways that will enhance what you are saying in your script. If you can add gestures to this that encourage focus, even better!

Improving Your Non-Verbal Sales Communication

It is clear that non-verbal communication needs to be a top priority for all sellers that want to learn how to become non-confrontational direct sales people. Improving your skills means taking the time to learn each movement, what it means, and how to use it in the right situations. That way they become tools in your sales arsenal.

There are many things that you can do to improve your non-verbal communication with other people. First, conduct a self-analysis on your appearance, or ask someone else to do it for you. Without fail, the first non-verbal cue is always what you wear and how you look. Your dress code matters because it creates your persona in the mind of your customer in seconds. You need to wear clothing and look the right way that matches the industry and the type of person you want to portray. Be mindful of tattoos, earrings, body piercings and other similar items. Tattoos are great if you are selling custom-made choppers, but they should not be highly visible if you are selling investment products, home security, insurance, and other in-home services. Wear the right clothing, and physically look like you fit the job.

I strongly suggest filming yourself practicing your script with a buddy so that you can see where you go wrong. You will be surprised to see how many times you confuse what you are saying with facial expressions and how your eye contact can dwindle. At the same time, you cannot change what you do not know or are unaware of. Watching yourself on video gives you the ability to actually "see it."

After three years of selling home security systems with non-confrontational sales theory and non-verbal communication techniques, Dan has become a master of meaning and showing what he says. As a result, he is in tune with the people to whom he sells, and he is in tune with himself.

After three years of selling home security systems with confrontational sales, Joe still cannot understand why his pitches work on some days and not on others. With only his verbal pitch to rely on, he is ignorant of what he is really telling his customers every day.

The difference here is an acknowledgement of different types of communication and a willingness to learn how to optimize, exploit, and harness it for sales.

Chapter 5

META-VERBAL COMMUNICATION

"To effectively communicate, we must realize that we are all different in the way we perceive the world and use this understanding as a guide to our communication with others."

TONY ROBBINS

The third element of communication lies in the meta-verbal realm. With meta-verbal communication, you can build your verbal and non-verbal communication into a fluid, seamless pitch that works every time you use it. That is because this form of communication helps you understand that *how* you say something is usually more important than what you say.

Meta-verbal communication includes voice speed, intonation, word stress, volume, and pauses. As a discipline, this form of communication counts for 55% of your overall emotional impact during a pitch. That makes this the most critical of the three communication styles to master.

Voice Speed Control

Think about the many ways you could say a basic sentence and how it changes the meaning for the person listening based on all the ways you could say it. This is the art of meta-verbal communication in sales. The first thing you should familiarize yourself with is that voice speed control dictates who gets sales and who does not.

Many sales people, charged on adrenaline and pumped from their sales team meeting earlier that day, will fly into a customer's home and rattle off their sales pitch "like a pro" in ten minutes flat. The only problem with this is that they are ruining their chances of landing that sale. Telling is not selling, as they say.

The faster you speak, the faster the customer will tune you out and completely disengage from the conversation. Fast words mean that they will not understand what you are talking about, and as a result, they will purposefully make up any excuse to get you out of their house. This bad habit spirals the emotional bank account downward. This also creates confusion, the salesperson's worst nightmare.

No one in the world likes to be "talked at." This makes them feel like the pitch is rehearsed and pre-planned and the seller could care less about them as a person. You need to learn to speak slowly so that your customer can take in everything you say naturally. *You want to speak just slightly slower than is natural.* This creates a higher level of engagement and deeper emotional bank account deposits.

Dan (speaking slightly slower than normal speed): *If you take a look at this area here (takes time to point it out), you will see that you are not protected from typical invasion points. What we can do is add a motion detector here in this location, (pointing to location to create a mental image for the customer), which will alert you if an intruder bypasses this first line of defense....*

Joe (speaking in normal speed or slightly faster): *Looking at here and here, you need security to cover these vulnerable places. What we can do is add sensors and a box over here, which will fix that issue....*

In this example, Joe hurries through his pitch and loses the sale. Dan combines the right words with the right voice speed control to optimize customer understanding and create positive emotional bank account deposits.

Voice Fluctuation

Have you ever heard the saying "The wrong tone can spoil the message"? The human voice is a wonderful multi-faceted organ that has the ability to fluctuate and create "moods" around the words you choose to use. To the customer listening to your voice, how you say things using voice fluctuation says more about your intentions than what you say.

To use your voice for maximum impact, you must be ready to vary the way you say things during script delivery. Here are some different examples you can use to alter the impact you can have with your voice:

1	Suggestive Tones	5	Annunciation Variations
2	Affirmative Statements	6	Muttering
3	Declarations	7	Shouting
4	Assertive Tones	8	Whispering

The sound of your voice will help your customer understand what it is you are trying to tell them. If you learn to use it well, you should be able to build momentum and excitement about your product or service during the pitch. Focusing on the pitch, volume, rhythm, and intonation (the "sing-songy" part) of your voice allows you great control over the intended meaning of your words.

When it comes to sales, it is important that you make sure the vast majority (if not all) of your sentences end with your voice in a lower tone, *not* a higher tone. When you end your sentences in a high tone, it communicates a lack of confidence to your customer.

Think of a basic question that we can all relate to. Across the country, in every bar in America on a weekend night, there are millions of "dudes" hitting on girls. If an unconfident guy asks a girl, "Hey, can I get your number?" and ends his sentence on a high note with his intonation moving upward, does he actually get her number? No. Fact is, 99% of the time he does not. His voice shows a huge lack of confidence by raising to higher tones at the completion of his questions or sentences.

Then there is the guy that seems to hit it off with a bunch of different girls each weekend. He says, "I really need to get your number." His confidence has his tones ending downward, displaying ultra-confidence and certainty. And he gets her number! People are attracted to confidence (not cockiness—there is a difference). All people are attracted to this attribute. When you

> Repeat these two sentences out loud, ending each sentence in a high tone. Then practice ending the sentences in a low tone.
>
> *When your technician shows you the functionality of the home automation and security system, you'll see the value and benefits right away. I'm going to outline it for you right now so you can see why it makes so much sense to everybody I have talked to.*
>
> Do you see the difference? After you practice this, choose a sentence from your own industry from the new scripts you have created while reading this book..

focus on ending each sentence in a lower tone, you create an atmosphere of certainty, professionalism, and confidence.

Your tone contains the emotional message for your customer, which is why it is so important to check your emotions and personal life at the door before each sale. If you have had a bad day, you cannot let that be communicated in your tone. The feel of your message is more important than the words you have purposefully chosen for your script.

It is your job to psychologically arouse interest and create engagement in the mind of your customer. This is controlled by using the tone and voice fluctuations you will practice along with your planned script. A good start is to pick out several of your most high impact sentences in your script then test different tones to find one that will have the most resonance for your customer.

Having personally trained thousands of direct sales reps in door to door, in-home sales, and telesales, this is the number one attribute that top performers learn to utilize. Master it!

Word Pressure and Enunciation

With meta-verbal communication accounting for 55% of the impact that you have on your customer's emotional bank account, choosing which words to enunciate is a skill that can provide clarity to even the most complex of scripts.

Dan is given an enunciation exercise to improve his script delivery. As you can see below, each word that is enunciated (underlined in the example) creates a different meaning for the sentence delivered.

"<u>I</u> did not tell head office that you were not happy with the product."

"I <u>did not</u> tell head office that you were not happy with the product."

"I did not <u>tell</u> head office that you were not happy with the product."

"I did not tell <u>head office</u> that you were not happy with the product."

"I did not tell head office that <u>you</u> were not happy with the product."

"I did not tell head office that you were not <u>happy</u> with the product."

"I did not tell head office that you were not happy with the <u>product</u>."

The enunciation changes the meaning in each sentence:

Someone else told head office.

- I really did not tell head office.
- I implied that you were not happy.
- I told someone else you were not happy.
- I told head office someone else was not happy.
- I described it in a different way.
- I told them you were not happy, broadly speaking.I told someone else you were not happy

You should speak slowly and intentionally while ending with a low intonation and a soft tone. Once you have mastered this, it is time to pick out specific words in your script that you could enunciate, or apply pressure to, in order to increase clarity and improve impact.

It is amazing how this exercise can reshape how sales people place emphasis on certain words to clarify meaning. Dan has discovered that well-placed emphasis can communicate what he means quickly and easily to his customer.

The real power of the human voice is seen in this exercise as the words are identical but the meanings of each sentence are different—thanks to the enunciation. Generally speaking, you should practice stating every sentence of your sales script so that the words and voice patterns come naturally to you.

Bottom line—your communication must be controlled, and each sentence is *intentionally* said a certain way. There is not a single person in history that became number one or the best at their sport, job, or industry by "winging it."

Volume

While you are learning to control your voice, you also need to be aware that volume is a meta-verbal element that can be useful in your sales pitch. You can always gradually raise the volume of your sentence until you build towards a crucial final point. This can be powerful and a great way to close the deal.

Adjustments in vocal volume say a lot to your customer about the story you are telling. Monotonous volume and tone, for example, is an enemy for sales people everywhere. With an equal, monotonous voice, people quickly lose interest in what is being said. If you habitually fall into monotone patterns, you need to rid yourself of them to thrive in sales.

There are many nuances in your message, and this needs to be communicated through volume fluctuations in your voice. You must speak loudly enough for your customers to hear you but never so loud that they feel you are being noisy or rude. At the same time, you must avoid speaking too softly or your customers will strain to hear you and lose interest. *You need to speak with a lower volume than is natural.* They need to hear you of course, but speaking slightly softer will increase engagement and create a more impactful non-confrontational atmosphere.

Spacing/Pauses Between Words

The final voice fluctuation that you need to focus on exists between...words. The pause! Purposefully leaving a pause in certain parts of your script can invoke a specific response in your customer. The right pauses are especially good at the very end of your pitch, when you are trying to close the sale.

Customers usually feel slight pressure at this point, which you can use to your mutual advantage. As you practice speaking clearly, deliberately, and slowly you must never allow random pauses to happen—or they could ruin the meaning of your sentence.

You cannot under any circumstances use pauses after a soft close. Remember that a pause can mean "Do you want to buy from me?" if placed in the wrong location. Let's take a look at what Joe has been doing with his natural pauses and how they always lose him the sale.

Joe: *Have you thought of home security before?* ***Pause***

Customer's inevitable response: *You know…I am really not interested.*

A much better way to handle this situation would be Dan's method:

Dan: *Even though you have a safe neighborhood, I am sure that you have thought about home security before… just for the peace of mind that it offers…how many doors do you have that lead inside your home from the outside?*

Customer's response: *We have three doors….*

In the second example, Dan uses pauses to ask a non-direct question at the end of a statement that purposefully builds value and avoids objections.[7] The customer feels less threatened to respond to the question, and as a direct result, they are more likely to progress the sale by responding to the question instead of trying to force you out of their home.

Pauses should only last for a second or two before you move on to your next statement. Any longer and your customer's natural ability to detect falsehood will kick in—and they will hear you are staging a response. This is why you need to practice these patterns and pauses—so that they are 100%

---

7   Andrew Dlugan, Speech Pauses: 12 Techniques to Speak Volumes With Your Silence, http://sixminutes.dlugan.com/pause-speech/

convincing and natural when you use them. The only time you pause longer than one to two seconds is if you drop a hard close, which in non-confrontational sales theory is rarely, if ever, done.

If you learn to use pauses correctly, your ideas will be communicated more persuasively. Use them incorrectly like Joe, and your customer will struggle to comprehend your message. Pauses help convey emotion, they assist with the pace of your delivery, and they can draw the listener into your pitch. Use them!

Mind Over Matter!

In non-confrontational direct sales, these small speech inflections will add up and make the world of difference to your bottom line. Remember, the more positive chemistry you can save up in the brain and emotional bank account of your customer, the more likely they are to hear you out and eventually buy your products or services.

I like to think of the sales process and the emotional bank account as a large bucket of water that you need to fill to a certain level—before your customer will feel "more than half full" and will move forward with your proposal on the same day you deliver it. Each thing you say, and the *way* you say it, will add a drop of water to that bucket, or it will take a drop away.

One drop might seem like nothing to the untrained sales person, but over the course of a deliberate conversation with your potential customer, there are thousands of drops that will either fill or empty that bucket. Every single drop matters—emotionally, physically, and chemically of course.

You must learn to master these communication types in their entirety. This will help you control the faucet as you learn how to make larger deposits of water while controlling any leaks that may spring up over time. Getting the customer to listen, stay engaged, and understand what you are saying to them will make you a power seller. With these techniques, those buckets will fill up quickly!

When problems do inevitably arise, you must learn to overcome those situations and objections like a professional. If you do not learn how to do this, many of your opportunities will be lost because they tend to recur among different customers. In most cases, small issues will be irrelevant, and your water deposit will far outweigh any concerns.

Learn to work with industry associates or, if you are in a company, with other team members, and come up with a list of best practices. Then roleplay in your teams to try to understand the outside perspective and improve what you are doing. When it comes to transforming yourself into a master of non-confrontational selling, you have to believe in mind over matter.

I guarantee you that focusing on these meta-verbal techniques will give you a newfound confidence as you explore the amazing impact that they have on your customers. You can be the world's most convincing seller, but you need science and brain chemistry to do it. You must be intentional and methodical about your communication.

Improving Your Meta-Verbal Sales Communication

Ignore meta-verbal communication at your own peril! A competent non-confrontational direct seller believes in the strength of science to control meaning in the messages they create for their customers. That means practicing hard on your tone, voice volume, pauses, enunciation, and speed.

These are not "add-ons" to your existing speech development abilities. To prove this fact, I want you to get a video camera and perform your current speech with a friend so that you can rightly analyze the responses and how you performed on a meta-verbal level. Just an FYI—less than 1% of the people that read this book will do the video. Those individuals will double their sales. They are the "doers." Be a doer.

Then I want you to sit down and comb through the video, writing a report about every inflection, tonal change, or pause that could be improved. I bet you will be astounded at how many times you misled your customer with a wayward tone or incorrect volume use.

Meta-verbal communication works in conjunction with verbal communication to create an effective method of verbally approaching your customers to close the sale. When you learn your script this way, you understand more than just the words that have to be said. You also understand the message that you are driving through to your customers.

Time and time again, a clear non-confrontational message using these techniques will result in more sales, higher conversion rates, and long-term paying customers that are happy with your service. Good news will get out about you and your brand, which means more opportunities to sell—to neighbors and anyone else that would like to hear it.

Consistency in communication leads to consistency in direct sales.

In three years of selling home security systems with non-confrontational sales theory and a combination of all three communication techniques, Dan has become a master of clarity and intentional sales communication that produces results. His conversion ratio is so high that he consistently wins awards in his company for excellence in direct face-to-face sales.

In three years of selling home security systems with confrontational sales, Joe is still struggling to create scripts that work. He has no idea what he is doing wrong and does not understand why some people in his company do well while he hangs on by a thread.

The difference here is that Dan is focused on optimizing a proven technique that is based on science, while Joe is using the same old sales techniques his father used 50 years ago. These techniques are outdated and disastrous, and they do not produce consistent results.

Chapter 6

COMMUNICATION OVER THE PHONE

"As we grow up in more technology-enriched environments filled with laptops and smart phones, technology is not just becoming a part of our daily lives—it's becoming a part of each and every one of us."

ADORA SVITAK

I want you to hit delete on everything you think you know about cold calling. Remove the very word from your vocabulary. While many sales books are still trying to teach people how to bully sales out of their customers, non-confrontational sales people use a different approach. I am pleased to report that with the newer methods, you get a better result 100% of the time.

Imagine that! Phones have become *more* important, not less important. Do not confuse this with the bad reputation that the modern call center agent has been given. With appropriate, science-based phone etiquette that is non-confrontational, helpful, and direct, you can secure more sales this way than you ever thought possible.

Repeat after me: *My phone is my friend.* There is no shame in knowing how to correctly use a phone to improve your sales!

Modern Phone Etiquette

We live in modern times when there are often several smart phones in your customer's family. Having someone's home phone number can be enormously powerful, and it is a gift in this cluttered day and age. You want to make sure that when you call your customer that they do not mind talking to you at all.

That means focusing on relational interactions, which emphasize the importance of how people are treated in the process of achieving results. The old method used transactional interactions, which focused more on the results and aimed directly for that outcome—which used to make people feel devalued, harassed, and irritated.

Here is the list of new relational phone etiquette tips that Dan received at work:

- Listen carefully. Listening helps you understand how your customer feels. Good news or bad, your first goal is to let the customer talk and validate how they feel. Ask follow-up questions, and adopt a "tell me everything" attitude.

- Show appreciation. Thank your customer for being honest, and tell them that you appreciate it when customers let you know when things are not right.

- Show empathy. Always apologize for any inconvenience, and validate their feelings using statements like "I don't blame you" and "It sounds frustrating."

- Always answer your phone in less than three rings maximum. Availability is key to customer service.

- Always answer with the same rehearsed greeting to inspire familiarity and consistency.

- Look up the customer's account, and thank them for being a valued customer.

- Always ask permission to place the customer on hold.

- Transfer calls by saying, "It is my pleasure to connect you."

- Before you hang up, review everything that you discussed, and restate any commitments you have made to the customer.

- End your phone call with the same consistent goodbye.

- After the call, make notes about items outside of the service you offer. Ask about those items on your next call. (Example: "How was that trip to California you were planning?")

New Call Center Laws to Follow

The modern-day call center needs to conduct good business, have friendly operators, and have well-written scripts. These all serve the company's bottom line. As the years have rolled by, new laws have become important to implement so that you do not harm your business with telesales instead of improve it. Bad practices have led to customers' pathologically hating telesales staff to the point where they go on national "Do Not Call" lists.

For non-confrontational direct sellers and their call center teams, there are many rules that must be instituted for strict control of their customer service. There is simply no point being excellent in person and then referring your customers to a rotten call center experience.

- Do not allow your call center staff to hurry through calling long lists of numbers for hours on end. You have to stop being busy so that you can talk to people long enough to understand them and for them to understand you to close deals. Period.

- Some 85% of available new business goes to 5% of the people willing to talk to the same customers again and again and again. Those 5% do not harass though. They set up the right calls and callbacks with the right information and methods.

- Calling is a quality game, not a numbers game! This has been proven repeatedly by modern call centers that practice these new laws.

- You should focus on getting more information on the people you are calling. The more information that you have, the higher your conversion ratio will be.

- Do not shorten customer names or make assumptions about nicknames. If they are Richard in your file, do not assume you can call them Rich or Dick. And trust me, the "Dick" example has happened many times.

- At the same time, do not react to strange or unusual names. If you say a name wrong, just apologize and move on. Or ask for help pronouncing it. The key is not to make a big deal about it. With a name like Babe, I can assure that it gets really old.

- Never ever say, "I want to take a moment of your time." This alerts the customer to the fact that you are already taking something from them.

- Never use the phrase "saves you time and money," because they do not hear it. It is way overused in sales pitches.

- People buy for their own reasons, not for yours. Remember that telesales is all about the person you are talking to, not about you.

- Appeal to your buyer's personal needs, and motivate them to gain something and also to avoid the loss or pain of the problem you are trying to solve.

- Ask the customer for help, and make sure that you understand your primary objective for the call before you make it.

- Rejected or not, you should always leave the customer feeling good about your interaction and the company.

- Try to get each customer to join an email mailing list by inviting them to be a part of your network that receives tips on something specifically valuable that you deal with.

- Every day that ends in a call or a door knock is a win.

- Do not apologize for wanting to help your customer, and do not thank them for taking your call.

The Call Center Bible

To become a good sales person, you need to sharpen your telephone communication as one of the vital skills on your road to success.

Telemarketing, or telesales as you may know it as, has become one of the largest and fastest forms of selling globally. There are thousands of organizations that offer numerous products over the phone to their chosen market. To be effective at phone selling, you must be mature, be responsible, and have a strong desire to succeed. Most of all, you must be aware of the latest practices that are working in the field of telesales.

To help you navigate this often confusing communication strategy, here are some commandments that will get you through non-confrontational telemarketing.

- When you call a customer, first gauge their tone, and then hear what they are saying. This is what they do in order to respond to you. Practice recognizing voices that are anxious, nervous, bored, confident, excited, or relaxed.

- The key to being a master of non-confrontational calls is to be relaxed and speak confidently to your customers with perfect verbal and meta-verbal communication skill.

- Watch out for the pushing people, and focus on pulling them by using tone, pauses, inflection, speed, and word choice. General sales resistance will happen. No one wants to be "sold," but everyone loves to buy something of value.

- When resistance happens, you must learn to pull the customer in, not push them towards the sale. Here are Dan and Joe to illustrate it:

> ➤ **Joe, using push:** *We need to get you scheduled right away because this is a limited time offer and the products are going fast....*

> ➤ **Dan, using pull:** *Obviously there are a lot of people trying to gain access to these services, so let me see if I can squeeze you into the schedule as soon as possible....*

Can you see, and more importantly "feel," the difference between Joe's pushing and Dan's pulling? This is a huge difference for the emotional impact on the customer's EBA!

• Maintain your Do Not Call list procedures and respect them. You must do it the right way for long-term success. No shortcuts!

Beating the Call Back

How does a non-confrontational sales person beat the call back before it happens? Often while speaking to a customer, they will dismiss what you have said, and they will tell you that they would rather you "call them back." Realistically, these call backs produce very little sales because the customer never has any intention of listening the second time around.

That is why you need to learn how to beat the call back before it kicks in.

These techniques will help you avoid the "call back," which never seems to materialize, or if it does, you are simply blown off again. Avoid it up front with smart non-confrontational techniques, and you will close that sale.

- Always put feeling into your sentences using your skills with tone of voice. Using something different will help humanize you to your customer:

  1. Dan: "How is your Wednesday treating you so far?"
  2. Joe: "How are you today?"

- Begin with an introductory ending by saying things like "This call is to see if we should talk further" or "To see if you qualify for the program...."

- Once you have moved your prospect from the point where they are receptive to hearing you, continue with recommendations, not pitches. "Based on what you have told me, I would definitely recommend seeing if you qualify for the consultation. Let me see if I can squeeze you in..."

- Keep social proof in mind. People are more influenced by the actions of others than by anything you could offer them.

- Never agree to make a follow-up call until you have gotten the homeowner to commit to doing something between then and now, or you will lose the sale. For example, if you sell energy efficient lighting, you might ask them to count the number of bulbs and their wattage in the house. This is something simple that anyone can do, and that gives everyone information that progresses the sale.

- Always schedule your appointments for the closest and absolute next time you can call them. The information must stay fresh in the customer's mind. Your prospects will lose 50% of the information you tell them every 24 hours that goes by. That is why they say "time kills all sales."

- As a last resort, set the call time, and try to make it for a call later that day. Then call them back at the exact time you confirmed.

Numbers Game Training

As a non-confrontational direct seller, you need to focus your time on your own unique abilities and responsibilities. The secret is out. The more you enjoy something, the more focused you become on doing that thing well. And the better you get, the more you enjoy it! Excitement is a natural product of being profoundly focused on something that you love and are getting really good at it.

No one in the world is born a professional athlete. They were once kids on the playground that found they had a natural talent for a sport. Then, after years of practice and focus, they finally become the best as they join the big league players. The lesson here is that focus can determine positive outcomes if you dedicate enough time to it.

When I train sales people, I ask them what it means when I say, "It's a numbers game out there." I love hearing the responses of "the more people I talk to, the more sales I get." BS. We all know that is not true. You can talk to millions of people and not sell anything at all. Mastering the numbers game is this. The more people I *engage* (not just talk to) that *understand* my message, the more sales I will get.

Let's use outbound phone calls as an example. For easy math, we will say that you are going to make 100 phone calls in a day in your outdated calling style. At the end of the day, you get seven people (probably by luck) to engage, and you set two appointments.

Now...the new you decides to do *focused* calling instead. Your objective is to get as many people to engage fully into the conversation and *understand* your message as possible. You focus on slow and low voice control and create a non-confrontational atmosphere that allows for people to engage.

You only make 60 phone calls in the day, but you have 21 people who engaged with you. And better yet, because they understood the message, you set 15 of the 21 appointments. Does it not make more sense to focus on people you engage than people you call? Of course it does.

Dan has been taught to center his small talk around general commonalities:

- City in which they live

- Current events

- Interesting weather, *not* regular weather! People hate talking about boring weather!

- A unique sports event

- Family that lives there and is interesting (not "Oh, my mom lives in California!" No one cares about that, believe me.)

Learning to Make Small Talk

Small talk can be the most difficult thing in the world to learn if it does not come naturally to you. However, if you break it down, it is not as scary as people believe. Small talk is really about finding things in common with your prospect without them feeling like you are wasting their time. This can be tough to learn, but it makes phone conversations a lot easier.

Nobody wants to sit on the phone speaking to a salesperson who is wasting their time. If you have something authentic and real to add, then talk about it. No topic should be discussed for longer than about 15 seconds, or your prospect may become irritated.

Keep in mind that small talk is about establishing rapport, so it is not supposed to sound like meaningless "filler." People will hear your disinterest and eagerness to begin a sales pitch, and they will dislike you for it. Good small talk puts your listener at ease and helps them listen to you!

Trial Closes and Tie Downs

Trial closes are questions you will use to test the waters with your customer. You want to find out whether or not you and the customer are in agreement. In non-confrontational sales, a trial close can be very transparent. Let's see how Dan uses it here:

Dan: *We've visited for a while today. Let me stop and ask you a few questions to see where we are.*

This "reassessment" is called a minor close or trial close because it seeks a smaller decision from the customer before the final commitment. You would say this to test the waters and then continue based on your feedback.

You would *not* say, "Would you like to move forward with me today in this new program we are offering?" This is a direct close. Instead, shape it like this:

Dan: *Does that make sense how we get you discounts by helping us out with some referrals and additional exposure to new clients?*

Trial closes are tests of your growing alignment and familiarity with your customer's needs and wants. The feedback that you get will help you determine if you are close to the final close, which can come at any time.

Tie downs, on the other hand, are phrases that ask for confirmation.

Dan: *Wouldn't that be great?* or *Can't you, isn't it, wouldn't you?*

When you ask for agreement and you get your customer into a pattern of saying yes, it leads to a sale. Dan, for example, might say:

Dan: *It would be great if I could get you the full marketing discount, wouldn't it? Here's what we need to have ready in order for that to happen."*

To Recap:

- Use phone etiquette to focus on relational interactions in order to engage and convert your customer. Learn the 10 phone etiquette tips.

- Call center practices are important. Understanding and quality trump numbers and speed during the calling process.

- Telemarketing is among the most difficult methods of selling, but it is also the largest and fastest way to sell when done right.

- Remember the six commandments of non-confrontational telemarketing.

- Learn to beat the call back by mastering tone of voice and humanizing your pitch. If you agree to a follow-up call, make sure the customer has to do something for you between now and then. Schedule appointments for the next available time slot possible.

- Non-confrontational sales is not about talking to a lot of people; it is about engaging people and helping them understand your information clearly.

- Small talk can be a powerful tool. Stick to the six rules of creating positive small talk so that you can establish rapport.

- A trial close tests the waters with your customer to see if they are ready to say yes.

- Tie downs are phrases that ask for confirmation.

Section III:

FROM TECHNIQUES TO CLOSING: NAILING THE SALE

Chapter 7

ADVANCED DIRECT SALES TECHNIQUES

"Do you want to know who you are? Don't ask. Act!
Action will delineate and define you."

THOMAS JEFFERSON

How do you, as a non-confrontational direct seller, "nail the sale"? Understanding the ins and outs of practical non-confrontational selling is key at this level. That means knowing each advanced technique so that you can use them in the field. Using these prime techniques taught in this chapter, you will learn to convert your average lead into a sale every time.

These are the top shelf, practical techniques that the best non-confrontational sellers use in their daily strategies. Learn them, practice them, and perfect them by adding in your own unique flavor. These tools and techniques will help you close the deals you start, which means bigger, better sales days for you.

The Engagement Equation

In the realm of stronger communication, one factor sticks out as instrumental when dealing with your chosen customers: engagement! When you know how to correctly engage your prospect, you are able to physically and emotionally involve them in the sales process.

Your customer's sales experience[8] is based on how well you are able to engage them in conversation and establish a social connection.

ENGAGEMENT TIPS FOR IMPROVING CUSTOMER EXPERIENCE:

- Eye contact is important. Notice how your customer responds to it.

- Make sure that your speech is slow and low, as we learned in our meta-verbal communication training.

- Be aware of what is going on with you and with your prospect. If they seem in a hurry, help diffuse their nerves and verify time-constraints.

- Ensure that all distractions around you are off. That means turning off televisions, turning down radios, going into a more private room, placing your cell phone on silent, closing your laptop, etc.

- Be aware of the noise level around any kids. It may help to sit within eye line of the kids but some distance away for decent discussion to take place.

---

8   Bob Thompson, Customer Experience vs. Customer Engagement – A Distinction Without a Difference?, http://customerthink.com/customer-experience-vs-customer-engagement-a-distinction-without-a-difference/

- Try to ensure both people are 100% alert and attempting to understand each other. Questions come from both sides. Body language is in sync. There is a general feel of connectedness and fluidity.

How do *you* feel when you are engaged with a customer:

_____

_____

_____

_____

Qualifying a Customer

In direct sales, qualifying a customer is a set of techniques used to determine if a certain lead has specific characteristics that might qualify them as a prospect. In other words, it is your job to figure out whether or not the potential customer will buy from you. In non-confrontational selling, you need to understand that the process of them qualifying (and needing/wanting to qualify) is what drives the majority of the actual desire. It is both a tool to qualify and also a technique to sell.

Think of the old eBay slogan: "It is better when you win it."

For some reason, when we bid on items on eBay, or any similar model, we check our computers and phones 200 times a day to see if we actually won the object we were bidding on and trying to get. Even if we end up paying the same price for it later on, it just feels better to win it.

Qualification works the exact same way. As people feel the need to be selected or qualified for something, the urge to have it gets stronger. Everyone has heard that people want what they cannot have. By having a qualification process in your sale, you create need, urgency, and value. This is a top-tier skill for advanced non-confrontational sales people.

Here are some tips to think about and some qualifying examples:

> **Joe creates no value and has no qualifying component in his sale:** *We're offering this great promotion to everybody because we really want to sell as many systems as we can.*

> **Dan creates value and a feeling of qualification to support his product's value:** *We're only offering this promotion to select people that fit the criteria and can truly benefit from our services. Not everybody qualifies for it. Let me ask you a couple of questions to make sure we are good fit for each other....*

It is easy to see that the qualification component is a catalyst in building value. Please remember that it must be authentic and real. Do not say things that are not true just to create this feeling. It needs to be genuine—people can feel the difference. That means create and implement actual policies that foster this qualification atmosphere and make them real!

Assumptive Language & Examples

Assumptive language can be a powerful technique to use in your non-confrontational sales process. This kind of sales language assumes the customer will buy and does not leave any room for doubt on that fact. When coupled with non-confrontational communication skills, it will not come across as pushy.

A buyer–seller relationship is often push and pull. When

you as the seller use assumptive language, you place yourself in a position of leadership and authority. Most of the time, a customer will go along with what is being said because it makes practical sense.

So when is the right time to transition to having assumptive language? You obviously cannot walk into the presentation and talk to them as if they have already bought the product. The right time to begin communicating assumptively is just after the qualification component of your sales process has been met.

Assumptive language is strongest when using assumptive timeframes and possession.

Dan's assumption: When *your home consultation takes place, you will want to ensure...*

Dan's possession: *When your home consultant arrives...*

A few more examples might be:

"They will bring you your information guide..."

"You will really like it when they... That is one of the program's best features."

"When your home qualifies..."

"When you get your upgrades installed..."

"When you get your custom-made..."

Here is an example:

"Let me ask you a few questions to see if you qualify for our program and to see if it makes sense for both of us to move forward."

After the questions are all answered:

"Based on what you told me, it looks like you're an ideal candidate for the program. When your installation takes place...."

The "when your" is the beginning of the assumptive language kicking in.

The goal with assumptive language is to help the customer visualize and accept that the product is already theirs during the sales pitch.[9] Here is an example of Dan using assumptive language, while Joe does not.

Dan: *We will have **your** security upgrade up and running in just two to three hours. **When** your install is complete, I will call and confirm it with you.*

Joe: *All of our security systems are quite extensive. So if you guys move forward, we would need four hours for the guys to come in and install everything.*

As you can see from the two examples above, Dan is using assumptive language to close the sale, while Joe is not. Using timeframe and possession, Dan ensures that his customer follows through with the sale. Joe's customer, however, feels negatively about the four-hour install because of how Joe framed the information. He does not close the sale.

Pleasant Persistence & Examples

There is another important technique that can help bolster your sales when you are face to face with your customer. There is a natural "sales resistance" that we develop very quickly as human beings in a world full of products.

No one enjoys "being sold" on anything, but everyone loves to buy something of value. The only difference between the two is framing and approach. Hard sellers are pushy and arrogant

---

9   Doug Fleener, Successfully Using Assumptive Language, http://customerthink.com/successfully_using_assumptive_language/

and attempt to force the buyer to buy. Non-confrontational sellers are helpful and friendly, and they do everything they can to get the customer to understand the product.

The classic difference here lies in the push and pull of the message being communicated. When people bring this resistance up, you need to learn to PULL a customer instead of PUSH them. These ideologies are exact opposites, so do not confuse them.

PULL: Places positive emotions in the emotional bank account

PUSH: Places negative emotions in the emotional bank account

Dan uses PULL: *Obviously there are a lot of people trying to get access to these programs, so let me see if I can squeeze you into the schedule as soon as possible.*

Joe uses PUSH: *We need to get you scheduled right away because this is a limited time offer and the products are going fast.*

The difference here is subtle, but to your customer, it is major. Joe's method makes your customer feel pressured, uncomfortable, and pushed into something they do not want. The very nature of the method means that they are pushed along the sales process, not understanding it at all, until finally being "forced" to say yes, which actually means no.

Dan's method flips this around. It makes what he is offering high value, in demand, and exclusive, which invites the buyer to want the product after they have been carefully and thoroughly walked through the sales process. They understand, and now they need to decide if they want it. This statement helps them decide to want it!

There is one magical pull phrase that you *must* use as a non-confrontational seller. It is both non-confrontational and direct, which makes it extremely powerful.

The magical phrase is: "If you had to guess...."

Here is our man Dan's example:

Dan: *In regards to your security needs, are you more concerned about a fire or a break-in?*

Customer: *I don't really know; I haven't thought about it.*

Dan: *Well, if you had to guess, what would you say?*

Customer: *I would have to say a break-in. You know, my neighbor actually had a break-in about four years ago, and...*

Here is Joe's confrontational example:

Joe: *I'm sure you guys have been concerned about a break-in before, right?*

Customer: *Well... not really. It's a pretty safe neighborhood.*

Joe: *Dur dur dur dur....*

Lost sale.

The Principle of Time Pre-framing

Pre-framing is a technique used mainly in neuro-linguistic programming to bring the natural defense mechanism down. People become anxiety driven and stir crazy based on their preconceived notions of how long your meeting or demonstration might be.

The great news is that time pre-framing is one of the simplest and easiest things you can do, and it will instantly alleviate this anxiety. Think about it this way. Have you ever heard a knock at the door and to your dismay you open the door to find a total stranger dressed as a sales rep standing there?

Of course you have. We all have. Let's say the sales rep says: "Hi, you must be Mr. Smith. I talked with your wife on the phone. How are you?" Of course you say fine, although in your head you are wondering what your wife set you up for. As your wife comes down the stairs, she says, "Honey, I totally forgot, but I got a call from XYZ company, and they wanted to show us some of their XYZ services that they have."

What goes on in your mind? Something probably like—*Oh @#*&, I should not have opened the door. How am I going to get rid of this person?* Or *Man...I can't let my wife answer the phone anymore!*

This feeling is what creates anxiety. You have no clue how to get the sales rep out of your house, and you literally feel like they will be there all day.

You are not alone. That is how a lot of sales meetings start— even if they are not from knocking on a door! But this changes with proper time pre-framing. In that same scenario, what if the sales rep said to you, "Thanks for answering. I know your time is very valuable, and I'll promise not to waste any of it. I'll give you guys a one-minute recap of what we discussed on the phone and show you what we do. If you are comfortable with us visiting for nine or 10 minutes, you'll have a great idea if this is something that makes sense for you and your family. Fair enough?"

How does the pre-framing make you feel? It makes you see light at the end of the tunnel. You essentially tell yourself, *I can deal with this for nine or 10 minutes.* This allows you to drop the defenses, diffuse any anxiety, and engage in the conversation! That is exactly why pre-framing works so well. Easy and effective.

The Six Principles of Persuasion

It always helps to have your persuasive language skills sharp and ready for use in the non-confrontational sales arena. As psychology and marketing expert Dr. Robert Cialdini taught us, there are currently six principles of persuasion that you need to perfect to become a master sales person.[10]

---

10   Tom Polanski, Dr. Robert Cialdini and 6 Principles of Persuasion, http://www.influenceatwork.com/wp-content/uploads/2012/02/E_Brand_principles.pdf

DAN FOLLOWS THE SIX LAWS OF PERSUASION:

1. **Reciprocity:** You invest in your customer, and they become more likely to say yes.
- Techniques:
    - Get "special approval" from your manager.
    - Give personalized, unexpected responses—going "above and beyond."

Dan: *Let me see if I can move some appointments around for you. You guys would definitely benefit from this.*

2. **Authority:** You frame yourself as a leader/expert/ specialist for credibility.
- Techniques:
    - Mention your credentials and your extensive experience in the field.
    - "Tee up" the appointment for a higher close ratio.

Dan: *We are the biggest in the country and the experts in our field. We do about 85% of the projects in this area alone.*

3. **Liking:** Likability is super important to persuasion. They will not listen if they do not like you enough.
- Techniques:
    - Find common ground, be authentic, and be real. Be the same as your customer.
    - Give them authentic compliments that make them feel good.
    - Offer them cooperation towards future goals.

Dan: *My goal is to help you achieve your safety goals. I've never met a person who wasn't interested in total security for their families. My job is to get you there.*

4. **Scarcity:** Your time as a seller is valuable, and your customer needs to know that.

- Techniques:
    - ➤ Squeeze your customers into your schedule.
    - ➤ Always tell your customer what they lose if they do not act.

Dan: *People are really taking advantage of these assessments. I'm not sure how many more they will be doing for free for those that qualify.*

5. **Consensus:** People do and follow what others do.
- Techniques:
    - ➤ Make your customer feel like they should be part of a movement.

Dan: *About 2,000 people in your area have already qualified for this assessment, and many of those have qualified for the program as well.*

6. **Consistency:** Be consistent with your promises, and build adequate rapport.
- Techniques:
    - ➤ Small commitments often lead to bigger commitments.
    - ➤ Voluntary, active commitments in writing work.

Dan: *Great, just grab a pen and paper and write this down for me.... I will be calling back on Thursday at 11 a.m. to verify that I can get you qualified.*

Question-Based Selling

Question-based selling is one the most undervalued techniques in all of sales training. Learning to master the art of asking the right type of questions in sales is how the very best sales people in every industry get to the top. Before we jump directly into question-based selling, let's establish the "why" behind using questions.

We all know that the nature of direct selling and in-home sales can be difficult. That is why you have to be mentally tough: to withstand the rejection that will inevitably come. Rejection makes it hard to stay motivated. It is part of the human response. We also know that the average sale requires five closing attempts before the prospect is ready to commit. Some 90% of direct sellers never make it past the second attempt. Motivation is lost!

If I told you that every door you knocked or every prospect you called on was a sure thing, your motivation would skyrocket, and you would be out there working countless hours on closing deals.

Most sellers do not realize that they can actually control and influence the outcome of each person they present to. There are only two ways to do this:

1: You increase your probability of success with each sale.

2: You decrease your risk of failure.

What you need, then, are *questions* that can either help you succeed or help you avoid pitfalls that lead to failure. Questions reduce your risk of failure in a non-confrontational fashion by gathering data and information you need to influence the emotional bank account. Having that data allows you to guide the sale towards hot buttons—increasing your probability of success—and also lets you avoid problem areas—decreasing the chance of failure. That is why questions that get you real and usable information from a customer can make you a dynamic and powerful salesperson.

A Little Dating Example:

To explain this concept, let's use a common dating scenario. Dan spots a woman he likes, and after talking for a short period of time, he decides to use question-based selling to get a date with her. Instead of asking a direct, hard sell question like "Will you go out with me on Friday night?" he does something different.

This is because Dan knows the only two answers to that first question are "Sure, here's my number" or "No, I would never go out with you." Given that he may not have made enough positive emotional deposits in her emotional bank account yet, Dan chooses to reduce the risk of rejection by asking a different type of question. He asks, "Wouldn't be great to do something sometime?" This question gets a 90% response rate of "That would be nice." It is automatic because there is no real risk involved by giving a response, only a positive outcome, and people are pre-conditioned to respond to that question in a certain way. After she responds with that answer, Dan can now actively pursue further because he has drastically reduced the risk of failure and pre-conditioned her response.

It works the same way in sales. Instead of Dan asking, "Do you want to move forward with the home security system?" he asks, "Are you more concerned about a fire or a break-in, if you had to guess?" This gives a no-risk response for the customer and pre-conditions the customer's thinking towards moving forward with the service.

The person who asks the questions controls the conversation.

Establishing rapport is critical in question-based selling.[11] Questions do not work if there is not at least some groundwork involved. After establishing enough trust, then you ask your customer, "Can I ask you a question?" or "Did I catch you at a bad time?"

When you get a positive response from these questions, you have reduced your risk of rejection. The goal is to elicit positive responses from these questions. No one says, "No, you cannot ask me a question," or "Yes, you did catch me at a bad time" when they are asked properly and in a non-confrontational manner after a little rapport is established. The real power behind this advanced sales method is that by getting them to invite you to explain yourself, they have taken down the walls, and they are literally inviting you to share your information. That is a *totally* different atmosphere than the feeling of having to force the information down their throat.

As with any topic, there are mountains of pages of information on question-based selling. As cited in the example above, I recommend the book *The Secrets of Question Based Selling* by Tom Freese. It is a great book for all sales industries, and it is a nice complement to the non-confrontational skills you are learning in this book.

---

11 Secrets of Question Based Selling, http://www.johnbesaw.com/Secrets_of_Question_Based_Selling.pdf

---

AS A RECAP: DAN'S CUSTOMER QUESTION CHEAT SHEET:

➤ Ask appropriate questions to decrease your risk of failure.

➤ Ask questions that open the floodgates for you to share information.

➤ Ask diagnostic questions that make you an expert and help you gather real data about the customer to drive your sale.

➤ Make the customer curious so that they start asking questions and they have a desire to qualify.

Transitions

The next important technique that you will learn about is called a "transition."

Every critical step in a sale requires a *deliberate* transition. Getting from A to B smoothly in a transition can make or break your entire sale. Transitions are key to guiding and controlling any conversation so that you eventually arrive at your successful outcome. This does not mean that you have to talk the entire time, but it does mean that when you talk, it should be intentional.

Asking questions, making statements, and adding to that emotional bank account will move you from one transition to the next. There are two major transitions in sales:

1. Getting into the home or presentation area (demonstrating your product, meeting in person)
2. Starting the sales forms (closing the sale)

Every sentence that you speak should guide your customer towards your desired end result. This can be arranged into a series of small milestones that you can build into your sales script.

Here are some milestone examples for sales people that do in-home sales:

1. Knock on the door, and introduce yourself in a non-confrontational fashion.

2. Get your customer curious, and create engagement. Get them to ask you about something.

3. Create a qualification atmosphere that says what your customer needs to do to qualify.

4. Determine if they qualify, and non-confrontationally create curiosity inside the home as to where/what your service will change about their home.

5. Create value and need in a walkthrough about the home services and products they are qualifying for.

6. Build additional value, scarcity, consensus, etc., as you prep to transition to close.

7. Transition into the customer information and forms.

8. Use non-confrontational assumptive closing to fill out the customer application/forms.

9. Collect any payment/necessary items and information to finalize.

10. Recap the entire process, and remind them as to why this was the best thing they have ever done in their entire life.

These 10 basic milestones are just examples that your customer must pass through in order to guide the sales process to where it needs to go. You need to create your own unique milestones and target getting to the major transitions and script out how you get from step to step. What can you say? How should you say it? Once you have done this, memorize your steps and scripting. Again—no one in history ever became the best at something by accident. You want to be the best…then act like it. Be intentional.

A huge key to success here is remembering one thing. Your only goal is to make it onto the next milestone. Do not worry about any future steps. And you *cannot* skip steps. Even if they get excited and want to buy after two steps, you must complete each step in order to have the right outcome, create the right customer expectations, and make sure the customer understands everything before the sales process is done. Focus on the very next step and getting to that step until you arrive at the final step.

Be wary that the two major transitions can kill your sale. You must learn to gauge where your prospect is at by asking the right questions. Trying to push into a demonstration too early will be a "Can you leave me some information?" or "Now is not a great time" response. And closing too early is a "No, get out" type feeling that nobody wants. Remember, if they are not ready, more positive emotional deposits will help. These mistakes happen mostly at the getting into the home transition and moving into the sales forms (closing) transition. Following each step helps you successfully blast through the transitions. Master these steps, and you master the sale.

Let's take a look again at an example from our security salesmen and how they transition into the final forms (closing transition):

Dan's transition into the sales forms after he senses enough deposits in the customer's EBA: *I'm really glad I could get you qualified for the life protection and home automation program. You'll really like it. The next step is that I just need some basic information on who you want the command center to call in case of an emergency. Barbara, let's start with your cell phone number.* (Dan's eyes and pen are looking directly at the form to write down Barbara's number.)

Customer: My number is 555...

Joe's transition into the sales forms: *So now that we have covered the home security system features, how do you guys feel about moving forward today?*

Customer: *We'd like some time to think it over.*

Joe: *Dur dur dur dur...*

Lost sale.

A smooth transition can and will make the difference in being a regular old traditional in-home sales rep and an industry leader. The key is knowing when to transition. As you sense that the timing is right, you do not ask to move forward; you simply transition smoothly to the next step with confidence and non-confrontational communication mastery.

Customer Expectations and Balance

It is very important to ensure that you are constantly managing your customer's expectations, from the moment that you meet them to the close of the sale. There is a balance that comes along with non-confrontational sales, and it can tip against you at any time if you are not careful. Slipping from non-confrontational to confrontational is a nightmare that can happen to anybody if you are not paying attention.

From these door-to-door visits and cold calling, you will either get scheduled meetings with customers or will arrive at a cold call meeting on the doorstep of a potential client. From the moment you meet them, all of these techniques need to come into play.

When you use the telephone, you need to learn how to treat customers well so that they know exactly what to expect from you.

- Listen to your customer. Better listening means better understanding and connection. The need to be understood is the most important of all human needs. Do not be afraid to let your customer talk, reject you, or deliver bad news to you. It is your job to turn the conversation around.

- Appreciate your customer. Thank your customer for the time and energy they spend with you. Thank them when they point out flaws in your pitch, product, or service.

- Empathize with your customer. Never dismiss the frustration or irritation your customers feel but rather acknowledge it. Reassert your reasons for being there while placating them with empathetic responses.

Once you connect with a customer, it is your job to be in constant supportive contact with that customer until they decide to buy. After they buy, you should still attempt to manage their expectations or successfully pass them on to someone who can. Customer relationships come first in non-confrontational sales; it is never just about the sale.

You should also consider giving something to your prospects for free. This is a technique that has been used with great success in sales for many years, and it has a place in non-confrontational sales. There is no quicker way to build trust and value between you and your prospect than to give them something of value for nothing. This proves to them that you are there for their benefit.

The best sales reps in large companies always ensure that their customers' accounts are handled carefully and professionally. If they need to, they will "go to battle" for their customers to get them the best deal or to help them achieve their goals with the least stress and effort. An active direct seller works for their customer and makes the sales process easy.

*Exceptional and memorable sales rep tip: Immediately after leaving a customer's home, take out a 3x5 notecard. Jot down any critical information that is fresh in your mind that humanizes your relationship and adds a personal flare to your communication. Examples are kids' names and ages, pet names, birthdays, or big activities they may have mentioned that are coming up. The next time you talk to this client, make sure to ask about them. Paying attention to the details earns you a customer for life!

Chapter 8

OVERCOMING OBJECTIONS

"Success is the culmination of
failures, mistakes, false starts, confusion,
and the determination to keep going anyway."
NICK GLEASON

In this chapter, you are going to learn how to overcome the objections that you may hear from your customers throughout your sales process. Understanding how to casually and politely sidestep or amend the objection is important if you are eventually going to change that customer's mind and get the sale.

Overcoming objections is a vital skill that you need to develop as a non-confrontational seller. Rejection is part of the job, as you know. Here you will learn how to convert those objections into a continued conversation so that you have more time to store positive emotions in your customer's emotional bank account.

Understanding Your Customer

To understand a customer's objection, you need to step into the mind of your average person. Ninety-nine percent of objections are not objections at all. They are, in fact, cover-ups. Your average customer is busy with all the things in their daily life when you come knocking or calling.

Their first instinct is to let you know that they are doing a million other things and are not paying attention to you or what you want at all. People love to seem busy! They also love to create a little bit of drama to keep themselves entertained and create a sense of purpose and value.

A true non-confrontational seller can cut through the veil and get to the heart of the objection to find out what is really on the mind of the customer.

How many possible objections are there? The great part about our line of work is that there is only one objection. Always. No more than one objection exists in the entire world.

When a customer makes any objection, this is what they truly mean:

"Based on what you have told me and how you have made me feel, I haven't heard enough information, or understood enough information, to get me feeling more positively about you and your services than feeling negatively about them."

That is the only real objection that exists. This means that you need to find a way to get your information more clearly understood by that customer. It means that you must not accept their surface objection as defeat.

In regards to objections, what comes out of your customer's mouth is generally *not* what they truly mean. They are saying something that you need to discover and understand. A customer speaks with more than just a few words.

The Validity of Objections

Have you ever heard that "every sales rep gets objections" or "it's a natural part of the sales process"? I have even heard people say, "You should view objections as a positive thing." How did these people ever sell anything at any point in their careers? I understand that there are degrees of truth in what they say, but you are crazy to think that you cannot influence the number of objections that come up, the impact they have, and how quickly and efficiently you can overcome them.

You can definitely help control the number of objections and how to get past them or, better yet, how to prevent them in the first place.

Dan has a process to manage the objections he has to face. There are two techniques that are working well for him: sidestepping them and breaking them down.

- **The Side Step:** When a customer mentions their first surface objection, it is best to just ignore it and move on. They are usually just trying to get rid of you because you have not spent enough time explaining the value you are bringing into their lives.

Customer: *I really just don't have a lot of time right now....*

Dan: *I understand. I'll be super brief. Can I ask you something real quick?*

Customer: *Sure.*

Dan: *How many doors do you have that lead into your home from the outside? The reason I ask is that although this is a safe neighborhood, they are finding that almost 87% of the break-ins for these nicer homes are occurring through one of the main doors leading into the house. How many doors do you have entering your home from the outside?*

Customer: *Three doors.*

Dan: *Okay, great. They've had some concerns on the back doors specifically. Do you remember if your back door is a slider, French door, or traditional? And is it that one there...*

Dan successfully buys time to be able to build value, break down barriers, and display a non-confrontational feeling to engage the client.

- **Touch and Go:** When you remember that people say things just to get rid of you sometimes, it helps to buy yourself some time to get yourself into the positive side of the EBA. You need time to do this, and the "touch and go" gives you more time. This technique begins by acknowledging their concern (because ignoring it and sidestepping it did not get you the time you needed) and moving back into the qualification process. Then address the concern when they are further into the positive section of the EBA.

Customer: *I can't afford it.*

Dan: *I totally understand. Because there are so many options and our services are custom to your needs in regards to pricing, let's first make sure you qualify and that it makes sense for you. Can I ask you a question? You mentioned that...*

Dan touched on the objection and then bought himself time by moving into the qualification aspect of the sale to further build value and need. He does an excellent redirect at the end with one of our "magical phrases" of "Can I ask you a question?" Now he is back on script, building value, and intentionally following each step of his sales process. Dan will follow the steps, show value that the customer will see, and improve the EBA, and he will close the sale.

Objections will come up, especially during the learning curve of non-confrontational sales. You have to commit to being there 100%, no matter what happens.

Let's take a look at how Dan deals with objections when he comes across them.

1. First, eliminate the word "but" from your vocabulary. Using "and" instead of "but" will help you build rapport, and that leads a prospect to say yes.

2. Always empathize with your customer, and then ask them a question. Choose from "I agree," "I understand," or "I appreciate." Once you have done this, the process is easy. It moves like this:

   ➢ Agree > Ask > Assume > Resume

Example: *I totally understand what you are saying. Can I ask you a question? Is your family...*

Back to script!

3. Use the feel, felt, found principle. (More on this later)

4. Overcoming objections is not the end goal. Remember that these techniques are a means to an end. Would you rather win an argument or gain a customer? Lead your prospect to where they will buy from you!

Try developing some of your own :

Common objections in your industry:

" _____ "

" _____ "

" _____ "

" _____ "

" _____ "

Your Touch and Go Responses:

_____

_____

_____

The Four Quality Principles

In the world of sales objections, there are four quality principles that you need to remember. Incorporating these will help you respond quickly and without confrontation to nearly any objection that is thrown at you.

Spend some time working out ways to seamlessly steer your customer back to the original script that you have created by overcoming objections. It can take some time to get this right, but practice makes perfect.

Kill Objections First

As mentioned, there is truly only one objection that exists in sales.

"Based on what you have told me and how you have made me feel, I haven't heard enough information, or understood enough information, to get me feeling more positively about you and your services than feeling negatively about them."

This is the reason the customer does not want to buy. It is your job to not reinforce that objection but to change it.

You need to keep it simple because objections are not a big thing unless you allow them to become big. If you talk on and on about something, your customer will feel like you are covering something up or that you are trying the hard sell.

Be simple and direct, and then, most importantly, move on! The most critical part of overcoming these objections is that when you finally overcome an objection or transition past one, do not sit there and dwell on it! Redirect and move on. Do not keep adding fuel to the fire that took you time to contain.

Even better than overcoming an objection is to beat an objection before it comes up. You can do this by being aware of your sales results and what is occurring at each of your sales meetings. If you are getting the same issue over and over again, redesign your script and pitch, and beat the objection before the customer even mentions it.

Here is an example of Dan redesigning his pitch to beat an objection before it comes up:

After two days in a neighborhood selling home security systems, Dan has tracked seven prospects that told him that they did not need his services because they felt that the "neighborhood is safe." Dan quickly recognizes this and does not waste any time adjusting his introductory scripting to beat the objection before it comes up.

Dan: *I'm glad we could use just seven or eight minutes to see if you qualify for the program we are doing. Your neighborhood is actually really safe. We are finding that most of our clients are trying to get access to the service for the peace of mind in that one-in-a-million chance something happens…and we are finding that they are loving the additional benefits from having home automation and home control features as well as the protection of the system. Let me ask you guys a few questions to make sure you qualify and that you are a good fit for what we do.*

Dan's Pre-Emptive Strikes Against the Objection

Let me start by saying I really respect you for taking the time to see these programs, and I respect you for learning about the new technologies out there to help keep your home and family protected.

I can't tell you how many times I have had an opportunity to enhance my personal situation and save money and I missed out on it. You folks are definitely miles ahead of most people.

> *I have talked to hundreds of home owners.... It seems like the smart ones are pretty decisive and learn to take action. They don't miss out on these opportunities.*
>
> *With your permission, I would like to do three things today:*
>
> 1. *Determine with certainty if you qualify for our program*
>
> 2. *Show you the programs that meet your needs and your own personal situation*
>
> 3. *Give you a roadmap on how this gets done in the quickest and most efficient way possible*

Dan has effectively beat the objection before it came up and non-confrontationally added value and justification to move forward and see if the homeowner qualifies for his service.

Here is another example of Dan pre-emptively beating a handful of objections during his introduction by placing value on the decision to move forward and look at his offering:

These examples get people to think less about "why not" and more about "this makes sense to me," which naturally reduces all objection possibilities. People are just people; they have the same relative surface objections and concerns wherever you go, regardless of what you are trying to sell to them. If you are losing control of the conversation at any time, you can use the "Can I ask you a question?" technique. This allows you to redirect the conversation back to your critical steps and start rebuilding your deposits into the EBA.

This will work every time, guaranteed. It is polite, and it puts the power back where it belongs: with you. From there, you can ask them anything you like and get the script back in play.

Chapter 9

CLOSING THE DEAL

"Obstacles can't stop you. Problems can't stop you. Most of all, other people can't stop you. Only you can stop you."

JEFFREY GITOMER

In non-confrontational sales, the close is still the most important transition that you will reach when you have executed your sales process. After all, without the sale, everything that you have done before means nothing. A seller is measured by the closes they are able to secure, so you need to learn how to master them in real time.

Closing the sale takes courage, timing, intuition, tact, and strategy. Smart sellers spend years learning how to "feel" the best time to initiate their closing transition. This is when you get the customer to transition into completing the sales forms together. Closing sales is a science and an art, and these strategies will help you make them happen.

Closing Techniques Explored

I like to tell my non-confrontational sales students that closing is like fishing. You continue to cast ideas out into the customer's mind, and you start to get nibbles and small bites. If they do not take the bait, then you do not close the sale and land the customer's account.

Keeping the customer highly engaged is the single best way to prep the bait and get them ready for the best possible cast you can give. Once you have gotten the client into the right mindset through non-confrontational selling, you know exactly when and where to cast your line. Older sales methods had you continue to cast over and over again until you had something finally bite. In today's world, you need to prep the bait and the hook and then cast your line perfectly to allow the customer to understand your message. Then, when your pole does begin to jerk, the fisherman has to give one final heave to set the hook and catch the fish. It is the same in non-confrontational sales.

You need to find your customer's ideal "bait" and use it to help close the sale.

The Art of the Close

Dan uses soft closes throughout the sales process to direct the flow of conversation and to gauge his customer's interest level. Without these soft closes, the closing transition will not work.

Using soft closes for the entire duration of the time that you spend with your customer is key. One method of doing this is to use ownership words. For Dan, it was concepts like "your new technology," "your program," and "your _____ (any benefit)."

When Dan uses ownership words with his customers, it helps them imagine owning his product, and they develop a sense of ownership before the sale is complete.

Dan uses soft closes like "Does that make sense?" and "Do you think this _____ (item) is better over here or possibly over here?" The customer's responses enhance his probability of setting the hook properly in his final closing transition.

The Five Types of Closing

Traditionally in sales, there are five main types of closing. If you can practice these and master each of them, it will help you close and solidify the sales you make with your customers. Let's take a closer look at how Dan uses the five types of closes.

DAN'S FIVE TYPES OF CLOSING

1. **Soft Close:** This technique helps your customer make small decisions that will lead them to eventually agree to purchase your product. It helps your customer envision themselves owning your product and is the basis for all other closes.

Dan: *So are you guys more excited about the more secure and efficient lifestyle you'll have or about saving money on utilities through home automation?*

Customer: *Probably saving money...*

Dan: *Great! That's what most people say.... The nice part is that this program does both.*

2. **Tie-Downs:** First you should lead your customers to a close with a series of easy, small "yes" closes that will amount to the big yes. Tie-downs can help you do this.

Here are a selection of Dan's favorite tie-downs:

Aren't they?	Don't we?	Isn't it?
Aren't you?	Shouldn't it?	Isn't that right?
Can't you?	Wouldn't it?	Didn't it?
Couldn't it?	Haven't they?	Wasn't it?
Doesn't it?	Hasn't he?	Won't they?
Don't you agree?	Hasn't she?	Won't you?

Dan: *Saving money while protecting your home and family would be pretty nice, wouldn't it?*

As you can see, Dan gets the customer to say yes with these tie-downs, which moves him closer towards an overall yes for the sale.

3. **Trial Close:** Use this hand in hand with your soft closes. This check will tell you where you are with your customer, like a system check. "Does this make sense?" is the most common version. If the customer seems confused, you should back up and retrace a few steps then ask again.

Dan: *Looks like you are a great fit for the programs we offer, and I'm really happy that we could get you the discounts we qualified you for. When your technician comes out, he will walk you through the options that the system provides for your home and family to get you guys the most out of your home-automation program. Does that make sense?*

Customer: *"Yes, it does."*

Dan: *Great!*

4. **Option Close:** One of the most powerful common closing techniques among the most successful people in sales is the option close. When used correctly, it will lead to a close the majority of the time. You need to be able to have smooth transitions so that when the time comes to close, you can transition through the close and the customer will progress naturally along with you.

Dan: *Looks good on my end as far as getting you qualified, and I can squeeze you into the schedule pretty quick here. Are mornings or afternoons better for you?*

Customer: *Mornings.*

Dan: *Okay, I can get you in for tomorrow at nine or 10 a.m. Which of those is best?*

Customer: *9 a.m.*

Dan: *Perfect.*

As you can see, the option close gives the customer two choices, both ending in a "yes," which means you close the sale. In this case, Dan uses "Are mornings or afternoons better for you?" This is critical in non-confrontational sales. You would never say, "So would you like to move forward with me today?" or any other ridiculous confrontational close. It will kill the sale.

5. **Assumptive Close:** A confident, authoritative approach works best here. You have to assume from the moment you start communicating with the customer that you are going to close the sale with them. You need to remain

calm and confident. Once you have finished your initial approach and explained your program, move directly into an assumptive transitional statement that casually moves the sale forward. This must be non-threatening, and you must use good meta-verbal tones with a relaxed and slow, soft speech for the customer.

Dan: *Great. When your technician arrives tomorrow, they will outline what we have gone over here. I'll squeeze you guys into the schedule since they are already working on a few of the neighbor's homes over the next few days. You guys are home tomorrow this same time, right?*

OR

Great. **When your** *installation technician comes out, I'll make sure he has the information we reviewed today. He's out here tomorrow, so I'll pencil you guys in for the same timeframe we had today. He'll only need about 2.5 hours to get it all done perfectly.*

(Continue on with traditional next steps—no need to ask for permission!

No Same Day Decisions!

What is the number one reason why an in-home sales person cannot close the sale? NSDD! This stands for "No Same Day Decision." Time is not on your side as a direct seller. You need to get your customer to move forward with the program on the same day you have provided the majority of your value building and presentation to close the sale.

Your success rate for re-pitching a person who instigated an NSDD when you "come back" (if you actually get back in) will be very low. With this in mind, there are two concepts you can use to overcome the NSDD objection. You can beat it before it arises, and you can beat it at the end of the presentation. You need to master both.

Here are Dan's best methods for beating the NSDD!

> ➢ **Breaking the Pact**

You can bet that nearly all married couples that agree to an in-home presentation have made a pact between themselves to listen but not buy anything at any price that day—"no matter what!" A big part of this comes from the nature of the appointment—one partner sets the appointment, and the other hears about it and will attend with this condition.

Therefore, to beat the NSDD, you must always "break the pact."

- Just after your initial introduction, but before you get into the presentation, you will need to do it. The break the pact script is simple:

Dan's Break the Pact Script: *John, based on what I know so far, it looks pretty good for you guys. That's great because not everybody can qualify for the programs, and not everybody is a great fit. If something comes out that might disqualify you guys from the program or that makes it not a good fit, I'll be sure to let you know so I can honor your time. I'm about to show you some information on the programs that only those like you (the pre-approved) are able to see. All that I ask is that after you both see the program, and they make sense to you and Nancy, you just give me a thumbs up or a thumbs down tonight*

---

if it seems to make sense for you in your own particular situation. Sound fair enough?

The format of this question is non-confrontational enough that 95% of people will say yes. This gives John permission to say yes or no. And true to non-confrontational sales, he gets to say yes or no based on how he feels at the end of the presentation. We know if we do it right, he *will* feel good about it, so all we want at this point is for him to feel like he has permission to give us an answer. After he says yes to this, at this point in "break the pact," Nancy will too.

With Nancy· *Nancy, can you also give me a thumbs up or thumbs down if this seems to make sense or not at the end? I'd really appreciate it. (After she says "sure" ...) Great! Thanks.*

Joe does not do a "break the pact" script at all, and after his presentation, John and Nancy, true to their commitment before Joe arrived, say, "Thanks for your time today, Joe. We never make a decision on the same day, so let us think about it for a few days, and we'll call you." John and Nancy never call back.

➢ The Trial Close

If they still resist in making a same-day decision at the end of your presentation, initiate a "trial" close. This softens the decision-making process and gets them to agree to "give it a try," which really means signing up for the program.

Customer: *Well, can you let us think about it for a day or two and we will get back to you?*

Dan: *Sure, that's no problem at all. I definitely want to make sure you are comfortable with everything as we move forward. Since the only homes we work with are matched up and qualified for the programs, I know you will definitely be very happy with it as my other clients here in this area are. If it seems to make sense and you really don't have any big outstanding questions about it, why don't you give it a try?*

Stay silent after this. The next person to speak is likely the one to concede. Quietly wait for the response. Most of the time, people agree to move forward with the program. If not, you are still in the *exact* same place you would have been before the NSDD. But this gives you one additional chance at closing the sale. The key here is that if you did the beginning right, pitched strong with non-confrontational skills, and created high engagement, it will not come to this point often.

Saving Your Bullets to Close the Deal

The next set of techniques that you need to learn about involve "saving your bullets." A bullet is a high value point that can be used to create a spike into the positive side of the EBA. This short-term EBA boost gives you just enough emotional response to push your sale through and to buy you time to continue building more and more value. If you find the sales climate declining—and the customers are losing interest—then you may need to bust out your bullets. Bullets are usually given away too early, thanks to the insecurity of the salesperson.

> ## Dan's Bullet Mindset and Strategies:
>
> ➤ You must believe that you are giving them the best deal.
>
> ➤ You must believe that they need your product.
>
> ➤ You must have pre-explained that it is such a good deal that you are limited as to what you can offer them but that you are confident it will help them in their own particular situation.
>
> ➤ Do not leave room for negotiation, or you will be pushed around.
>
> ➤ When the time comes, make them an exclusive offer ("squeeze them in," get them something "extra," and create a feeling of over-delivering that they will appreciate).
>
> ➤ Use third-party techniques to add value by "asking a manager" or "getting special approval." However, these need to be legit offerings and statements!

There is some debate over when to use your bullets in the sales process. Most people give them away at the wrong time. The wrong time would be before you have created value in your product or services or especially when they ask for it. Giving it away if they ask for it will instantly devalue your offering.

The best time to use a bullet is when you sense that they feel they are not getting enough perceived value for the perceived cost they are experiencing.

To illustrate this example, imagine going to buy a car and the salesperson that does not save their bullets says, "Thanks for coming in today. We are giving away a free tow package with every SUV sale." There is zero value built into that offering.

The non-confrontational and smart sales rep builds value through the entire sale, and at the end, to nudge the customer over the edge of the positive side of the emotional bank account, says, "I'll talk to the general manager and make sure we get you an upgraded tow package on your SUV today at no cost as well since this is such a great fit for your family. I'll just need some basic information."

Timing and delivery on your bullets determines the customer's perceived value of the bullets themselves. Do not give them away for free!

The Closing Timeline

All sales presentations have a timeline. You need to come to terms with this expected timeframe and learn to use it as effectively as possible in order to land your sale.

Focusing on the closing timeline means focusing on each of the milestones you created in chapter 7. It is critical to map it out and time how long it should take you to get to the major milestones.

This brief milestone timeline might seem basic to you, but a top-performing sales rep adds notes to it and develops it along with his practical skills. Top reps understand that they have a limited number of minutes with each customer to have them agree to the sale. As a result, these reps shape their script, know when and where they need to be and use the communication techniques to transition from one level to the next.[12]

The more information you can gather from a customer with the right questions, the more quickly you can find needs, build value, and move through the sales process. This is why top reps always seem to "get the easy sales." They have simply

---

12   Tracey Sandilands, Sales Techniques & Closing Scripts, http://smallbusiness.chron. com/sales-techniques-closing-scripts-24097.html

mastered their milestones and getting the best information through asking the right questions. So their sales are quick and efficient. They never waste time.

I have found that the single best way to find needs are by using a questionnaire style formatted survey. Start from general questions and move to being more specific. For example, you would never immediately ask a potential client, "How much income do you make?" But after a number of questions that are helping you design the best fit for their needs, that question becomes VERY appropriate at the right time without bringing in the confrontation.

After the needs are found, this is when you will add as many positive emotions into the customer's emotional bank account as possible throughout each milestone. Now that you have the information, you know how to guide each part of the presentation more efficiently. From there, the customer will begin to want your product. Once genuine want has been established, only minor objections are left to overcome. Then a smooth option close or assumptive close will wrap up the sale.

Under Promising, Over Delivering

Your under-promising, over-delivering technique will help you close sales. Many times this is trained as a technique where you purely want to deliver exceptional service so the customer is happy with what they purchased from you. This is obviously very good to do, but it is more than that. The best non-confrontational sales reps can create their own situations to over deliver by controlling the way in which they communicate. This is done by the manner in which they deliver any form of news. Let me explain.

If our "less than stellar" rep Joe is selling a service-related product that costs 50 bucks a month, he probably still uses his grandpa's selling technique by saying the following: "Well, Mr.

Smith, what I can do for you today is we have a truly amazing deal for you, and the price is just incredible. Today only, you'll be paying the great rate of $50 a month for this premium service." Blah, blah, blah. Sell, sell, sell. He has actually created a position for himself that the customer is expecting a very low rate, and if he is average or even decently priced in the market, the customer is going to be disappointed when he delivers the news.

Now let's look at our man Dan. Our non-confrontationally trained Dan understands that he can create a position at this pivotal point in the sale where he can actually over deliver to the customer based on creating a certain expectation before the information is given. Dan says the following: "Now, Mr. Smith, obviously this technology and service is the best out there. The tricky part with this high caliber technology is that it's expensive. We've seen people paying as much as $65 or $75 a month because the service and technology are worth that. The great part about getting you guys qualified for our program is we can get you into a discounted rate of only $50 a month. Can I ask you something? Did you know that...." (This question is asked here to transition directly into additional value building.)

Can you spot the difference? Joe leads the customer up to believe that the price is going to be incredible and then delivers 50 bucks a month, which now does not seem incredible because of the expectation he created.

Dan creates an image in the customer's mind that the technology is going to be very pricey because it is flat-out that good, but when he delivers the cost of only $50 a month, the customer will instantly think, *Well, that's not that expensive at all.*

Dan controls the expectation and the ability to over deliver.

The Customer Cooldown

Sometimes you get further by going slower. This means being in tune with your customer's emotions at all times. Customers are often swept away in the excitement of a good, well-delivered sales pitch.

Once the seller has left, sometimes it feels that all that remains are bits of paper and a new bill—which is why many customers have second thoughts. This period is called the "customer cooldown."

The single best way to prevent this is to give a recap of the entire sale. You must wrap that entire presentation and process up into a nice package with a pretty bow on it. They need to understand again exactly *why* they are moving forward with you and *feel* the reasons one more time in a simplified and non-confrontational fashion. Do not be afraid to use the language "Now let me just give a quick recap to make sure I didn't miss anything on my end. We were able to get you qualified for the XYZ program, which is the best program to qualify for. And what that does for you is…"

The customer will appreciate simplicity and a recap so that they can ensure they understand everything.

For those sales reps that want an additional, more advanced sales technique, you can add in a closing line to avoid cancellations. This is an advanced move specifically because if this is done wrong, you can totally kill the sale. But if done right, this will cut your cancellations in half. The pitch is as follows:

"Well, Mr. Smith, I'm really glad we could get you approved for this program; you're going to be very happy with it. Now obviously you and Nancy are very excited about it; I can tell just by our conversations. But the last thing that I want is to get a call tomorrow morning that we left something out or that something doesn't seem to make sense. Since I'm here now, and we worked so hard to get you approved today—and thankfully we got you approved—is there any last doubt or final question you have before I head out?"

If this is done right and you have presented with non-confrontational professionalism so your customers were engaged and understood everything, they will respond the exact same way every time by saying, "No, we are good on our end." This is a *very* deep commitment now and will reduce any next day cancellation calls by a huge percentage.

Reinforce Correct Decision Making

Webster defines "close" as "to put an end to; to finish." In sales, it pertains to the process used to bring your customer to a final decision via a logical progression of ideas that bring about a positive answer. The average close takes about four to five attempts to get right.

Everyone in the world has a tendency towards procrastination. One of the biggest problems that people have is making decisions—because of that, many things that could be accomplished never are. Decision making under pressure is even worse. People openly dislike being cornered and forced into a decision they may regret later on. This is why non-confrontational sales techniques are so powerful.

Your job is to provide your customers with sound logic and a progression of ideas that reinforce correct decision making. These correct decisions should all be about your product and how much value it will bring to their lives. Remember, the cost to value ratio must be considered at all times.

It is only too easy for the seller to get this wrong. You see a lot of people each week, and it gets tiring. But you are doing yourself and these families a disservice if you are not helping them decide to buy your product. After all, you believe in it.

And if you do not believe in it, this is your hint to not be a dummy and to find a new product immediately!

Often your customer may want security, for example, but because they shy away from decision making, they hesitate to make one at the end of your demonstration. But decisions are exactly what you need to close the sale. You must get a yes or a no. If you cannot get a yes or a no, the answer will always be no.

Time is important to you as a salesperson as well. You are only able to see a limited number of prospects and do not have time to waste. Restrict your visits to a specific time, and practice getting through your steps in a methodical and non-confrontational fashion within this time period. Most of us are aware of when we feel like a situation is rushed. It can be even more difficult to be aware of losing time and productivity through wasted communication. Both need to be managed to maximize results.

> Make it easy for your customers to decide to buy. After you have tested the waters with your soft closes, walk them through your closing transition. If you have done your job in a non-confrontational and engaging fashion, the only logical conclusion will be to move forward with you.

For you, correct decision making will always center around your customer buying your product. That is how much you believe in it and love it. Everyone should have it!

Learn From the Customers That Say No

Your customer is giving you feedback cues at all times during your pitch. You should come to terms with this information that they are communicating to you—verbally, meta-verbally, and non-verbally. I strongly advise that you practice closing with several people that you personally know so that you can get a feel for when you are losing your customer's interest.

The mantra "always be closing" is one to live by. As long as you keep your customer in the number one position and do not switch to the "push" selling style, you will be all right. Sometimes there is nothing you can do to get the sale, and the customer insists that they do not want to spend any money at all on anything new.

When this happens—after several techniques and attempts of course —you have to accept it. When this happens, make sure to always leave your customers on a high note. You never know if they will change their minds later. It also does not hurt to ask for feedback by saying, "Just so I can do my job better next time, what would have needed to have been different today for you to have chosen to move forward with me?" Let a "no" customer help you create more "yes" customers in the future.

> A strong close developed word for word over time and tested via multiple customers can be a huge asset in your non-confrontational sales arsenal. With every customer you use it on, ask for feedback like you are still learning. You will be surprised at what some people will tell you. Film yourself giving your close, and practice it over and over.

When you can use your expert close word for word after you have successfully prepared your customer and it works the vast majority of the time, you truly have something special. And as always, you will still have something to work on and improve for your own financial wellbeing. You can always get better and learn more. Always.

Specificity

There is a technique called specificity that will help you connect with your prospect and close the sale. It uses the art of being specific to engage your prospect and jar them out of an inattentive state.[13] When you have your prospect's attention, you are free to persuade them to buy using your prepared scripts.

With specificity you need to:

- Be direct and to the point.
- Be ultra-specific by utilizing useful, unique, and urgent language.
- Build credibility as you talk.
- Cut through the clutter by making the conversation relevant to your prospect.

Done correctly, you will hold your prospect's attention for the entire conversation, which means higher retention of information and understanding and a better shot of them feeling comfortable with closing the final sale.

Let me give you a clearer example that most people can relate to. We will use the bar example. This is going to be extremely cheesy, but it will get the point across. The typical guy in a bar will walk up to someone they have an interest in with very non-specific communication and a huge lack of confidence. Imagine saying to a person you want to take out, "Wow, you are beautiful. Can I buy you a drink?" Think of how basic and overused that feels, the environment you are creating (or not creating), and how you are making this person feel.

---

13   Chris Garrett, The Persuasive Power of Specificity, http://www.copyblogger.com/specificity-in-copywriting/

Now I will drop in some specific language and try to imagine the difference in the person's emotional bank account for how this has an impact on them receiving this information. "Look, I've been standing in that corner over there for 12 minutes trying to find an excuse to come over here and talk to you. I know this might sound like a line, but you are the most beautiful woman in this room, and I would love to buy you a drink. Would you let me do that?"

Whether you like it or not, you have to agree that the specific language used in this example creates a totally different level of engagement for your prospect. That is exactly what specifics do in conversation. Being specific is a volume dial that turns the engagement level way up.

So if we take our example to business, we can use just a few examples for non-confrontational in-home sales. Here are a few not so effective examples, with the more specific example that drives more power and engagement.

Less effective:

"Well, Mr. Smith, you have been a customer a long time, so I can definitely get you a discount on this upgraded service."

More effective:

"Well, Mr. Smith, since you have been a customer with us for six years and four months, that actually allows me to get you a discount on the upgraded service."

Less effective:

"So the good news is that we can definitely include taking care of your three kids as part of the service program you are signing up for."

More effective:

"Well, Bruce, the good news is that because you are qualified for the premium program, we can actually include Johnny, Susan, and William as part of the premium service program."

As you can see, you can change all sorts of your communication types to be more specific to drive engagement and get a much higher impact for all of your positive value points that will skyrocket your customer up the emotional bank account.

As a side note, this is obviously not just for business or picking up attractive people. This can be used to enhance any relationship and make you a dynamic person to be around. If you have kids, try it with your kids. Instead of saying, "Great game, son," try saying "Hey, Timmy, I saw you hit that ball just up over second base in the third inning. Man, you were sliding into second base before the guy even picked up the ball! Your hitting has improved, and your speed is incredible. You had a terrific game, son. I'm so proud of you." That example displays a dad who truly watched the game and gives his son the confidence and emotional high that will last a lifetime.

Being good at communicating is not just about making money. It is about having killer relationships. It makes a difference. No need to settle for an unemotional and low level life. Get specific with people!

Section IV:

BECOMING THE BEST: TRAINING, GOALS, AND RESOURCES

Chapter 10

SETTING SALES GOALS

"If you set goals and go after them with all the determination you can muster, your gifts will take you places that will amaze you."

LES BROWN

You have already learned a ton about being a killer non-confrontational sales person. All that remains is for you to round off your knowledge with some practical tips. In this final section, you will find out how valuable goals are to your process and how best to implement them for your empowerment.

Along with these final strategies, you will also be given access to a host of resources that you can use to better improve the way you plan, manage, and organize the way that you sell in a non-confrontational manner. With these resources and tips, you will be off to a running start on your road to becoming a high conversion non-confrontational sales person.

Basics and Goals

I once experienced a solid week of no sales from the top rep in one of my companies. It was clear that he was down in the dumps and had lost all focus. He asked me to come with him to some appointments, so I did. I told him he would do the talking and I would take notes; then we would discuss it afterwards.

At our first appointment, we met with a woman who lived in a nice house and was receptive to his questions. Then I noticed that the rep had pulled out his tablet and was trying to deliver the entire presentation from the doorstep. Since we were selling home security systems door to door, I interrupted him and asked the potential client a question about her back sliding glass door (a common vulnerability in security) that allowed us to enter the house and begin building real value and true engagement.

Together the three of us went in to inspect it, I continued the pitch, and within 90 minutes the technician was there to complete the install on a closed sale. When we discussed it afterwards, he admitted he had forgotten the basics—not even focusing on getting inside the house! His lack of motivation had taken him from being a top seller to a no seller in one week.

One of the biggest mistakes he made was not setting daily goals on basic items, like how many doors he would get into each day. These types of goals need to be set and reviewed daily, weekly, and monthly. With goals as a blueprint to performance, he would never forget the basics again.

The Sales Game Changer

I have always found the concept of a "game" a fascinating thing. Not only do I understand why it impacts the human mind like it does but I am equally as taken by the way that a simple game can produce astronomical results—even if the prize is insignificant.

Take sports as a glaring example. With sports "games," athletes dedicate years and years of their life training to become fine-tuned machines. They do it all because they want to win the match and be better than the opposing team or the other players.

People spend billions of dollars each year to watch these high performance individuals display their skills in these games of competition. They buy tickets, jerseys, hats, and memorabilia and tune in to the television when a game comes on.

Super fans even believe they are somehow part of the team! "We won!" they exclaim when asked how their team did. People believe that they have a role to play in these competitive games. Whatever it does to the human mind, it works!

People are willing to spend billions so that they can say, "We won," and feel good about themselves. The cure all for sales slumps, mediocrity, and complacency is to develop a similar game and integrate it into your work life. Create your own challenges, and then get other people involved. Maybe you lose the game, but you make twice the number of sales.

Whatever happens, you set yourself on a guided path to success when you see goals as an important game changer. A few years ago we created a "King of the Chair" game for one of our sales offices. The top rep of the day got to sit in this prestigious chair the next day during training. Everyone honored the game, and it was a massive success.

On average, those reps earned an additional $2,600 a month in commissions—all because they wanted to be "King of the Chair." A crazy idea, but one that worked. How can you develop your own games?

Try to involve your peers, your boss, and anyone that has an interest in holding you accountable. Goals can be games, and when you play them, you always win.

Accountability in Goal Setting

Goals only work when you are personally accountable and keep their integrity intact with hard rules. Why bother setting a goal if you are not going to keep yourself accountable?

There are many ways to make sure that you will stay on track when you set goals. Here are Dan's suggestions on how you should go about becoming a goal-master.

Dan's Rules for Accountability in Goal Setting

- Make sure that your goal is something you really want

It might sound good, but if it is not something you desperately want, you will struggle to find the time to make the goal a reality. Your goals must be consistent with your values.

- Make sure that your goal does not contradict any other goals.

You cannot, for example, buy a $750,000 house if your income goal is only $50,000 per year. Non-integrated thinking like this will sabotage your hard work. Remove these contradictions.

- Develop goals in all six areas of life.

These are family and home, financial and career, spiritual and ethical, physical and health, social and cultural, and mental and educational. A balanced life is best.

- Write your goal in the positive form.

Write down what you want so you can examine it and create an instruction list for your subconscious mind to

---

carry out. Give your mind positive instructions, and it will get the job done.

- Make sure that your goal is detailed.

Instead of simply writing "a new house," describe exactly what you want. How big is this house? Does it have a pool? What city is it in? How many bedrooms does it have? Be specific! The more information you give yourself, the clearer your final outcome becomes. Visualize each goal, and then describe it.

- Make sure your goal is high enough.

Set lofty goals that take you places. The higher you aim, the further you get. Ultimate goals can be broken down into smaller ones, but you will not reach one without the other.

- Review and adjust your goals.

Write down your goals to build your success roadmap, and then review these plans methodically. The more focused you are on them, the more likely they are to come true. Tweak and realign your goals along the way, but keep them top of mind to stay accountable.

Setting Non-Negotiable Goals

As a realist, you need to understand the difference between negotiable and non-negotiable goals. Why would anyone ever negotiate with themselves, you ask? There are lots of reasons in a high stress job like direct selling. Lack of responsibility, no integrity, and victimization are the most common pitfalls to watch out for.

Negotiable Goals	Non-Negotiable Goals
An unrealistic goal	A high but realistic goal
A goal with no ability to be measured	A tangible, measurable goal
A goal with no real timeline	A definite timeline for completion
A goal that you do not care about	A goal you are deeply passionate about
A goal that others make for you	A goal you empower yourself to take on

Here are Dan's Differences Between Negotiable and Non-Negotiable Goals:

Joe's Goal Examples:

- Save money by the end of the year
- Buy a big house with a large front yard
- Sell more accounts every month

Dan's Goal Examples:

- Sell 50 accounts this month based off the 45 I sold last month
- Buy a 2,000-square-foot, three-bedroom house with a pool by June of next year in Scottsdale, Arizona.
- Have $65,000 in a separate savings account by December 31 of next year

Daily goals can be even trickier because they can be easy to undermine. If you are not going to do them, do not set them! I want to challenge you to set your goals and share them with your sales team. Then set another four goals outside of these.

Goals:

_____

_____

_____

_____

_____

_____

_____

_____

_____

Four Personal Goals:

1._____

2._____

3._____

4._____

Chapter 11

HIGH PERFORMANCE HABITUAL SELLING

"The modern sales professional doubles as an information concierge—providing the right information to the right person at the right time in the right channel. Socially surround your buyers and their "sphere of influence": analysts, thought leaders, experts, peers and colleagues."

JILL ROWLEY, ORACLE

Habits can be extremely useful in the realm of non-confrontational sales. When you make being a high performer a habit, you start earning ridiculous commissions and will be on your way to becoming a direct selling industry leader. There is no overstatement here. I have seen it happen many times by using the techniques outlined in this book.

In this chapter, you will focus on your performance and how to get the most out of your job as a direct seller. It begins with your attitude and your ability, but ultimately these things can be improved and expanded on until you are a sales force to be reckoned with. It is time to adopt the healthy habit of being a high performance direct seller. Work begins now.

Elements of Performance

Personal performance happens when there are a number of predictable factors contributing to your success. I am at my best, for example, when I am being honest; when I believe in my product; when I am in good physical health; when I know I am doing well; when I have excellent discipline, hard work, and persistence; and when I can accommodate the moods of anyone that I meet.

Our man Dan has some advice for you in staying in peak performance mode:

- Keep a list in your pocket of one thing you can improve daily. Always only do one item to improve daily so you can truly focus on it. This is a hugely motivating practice!

- Find out the answers to all questions you get during your sales pitches, and write them down for review. Find the answers quickly, and adapt immediately. Learn them until they become a part of you.

- There is someone nice to meet every day that will want what you have to offer. It is your job to find these people.

- If you work harder and smarter than anyone else, then you will be more successful.

How will you make sure that you are performing each and every day?

Do Less, Get More Done

Before you embark on your non-confrontational sales journey, there is an efficiency principle that you need to understand:

Here is a reminder list of how Dan does less and gets more done:

- Slow down in every conversation. Time is important, so use it wisely. Slowing down in conversations allows for everyone to be on the same page, which saves time later.
- Learn to love saying the word "no" for the opportunities it presents to you. Saying a powerful no to useless time wasters and activities is you saying yes to your goals and to your success.
- Practice saying no to the people in the world that do not really matter, and you will have an easier time saying yes to the people that do matter.
- You must communicate until you are complete. You must ensure that all conversations are completed all the way through and that everyone understands each other perfectly. Define Who, What, How, and By When in agreements you make with everyone in your life.
- You must powerfully train leaders in your organization. Build up those around you. A strong team produces higher results for everyone. If others succeed, it does not mean you are less successful.

Doing less means focusing on your goals and motivations to keep you on track with laser accuracy. It also means delegating work that is not important, developing your team members to strengthen yourselves as a unit, and staying in touch with your own personal performance growth.

The EMPOWER System

Success is within your reach. Non-confrontational sales has taught you everything you need to know about handling people honestly and with confidence. To stay on the success path, use the EMPOWER system to realign your goals.

- ## E Is for Extrinsic Enrollment

Attracting a strong team is good for business, even if you are not a manager. Who are you going to attract to boost your own success? Express your commitments to these people, and help them keep you accountable. These individuals serve as extrinsic motivation.

Set daily, weekly, monthly, quarterly, and yearly goals that you honor because you have enrolled people in your success, have shared your goals, and have asked them to keep you accountable. Use this accountability to motivate yourself and your team to greatness.

- ## M Is for Mediocrity—and How to Beat It

There are loads of good direct sellers and good sales managers. There are a ton of good things in a lot of different companies. When did being good become better than being great? Most people stop when they are "good." This is settling for mediocrity. Never settle! Constant progression and always challenging yourself will allow you to beat mediocrity. You can always get better!

- ## P Is for Preparation

Being prepared helps you say no to everything in your life that is not in line with your goals. Distractions come when we do not have a well-defined plan, and they will corrupt you if you let them. Work hard when you must; play hard when you can. Plan both of those activities out, and define them. This is about success, money, and a better life for yourself. Decide to always come prepared.

- ## O Is for Optimism

  Staying optimistic is not just about thinking things will work out all the time. It is understanding that you have the power to make sure that they do work out. Optimism is about taking responsibility. Stop being a victim. Get your life figured out. You have control over the outcome and can always adapt and change. That is what being optimistic is about. Life happens. You can happen to life as well. You can fix anything.

- ## W Is for Work the Hours

  Direct sales is not a simple job. Even with all the tools in the world, you still have to show up every day and be your best, or you will not sell anything. That means putting in the hours—dedicating yourself to the daily grind. You will only master non-confrontational sales with actual work.

  I once knew a guy named Craig. He was not the brightest fellow I have had on a team. He spoke with a stutter, and there were obvious mental limitations that he lived with. But Craig did not care. People laughed at him and said he would never make it. Craig just did as he was told. He put in the hours and was in the top five for his office in the Midwest out of 30 sales reps purely based on working more than everybody else. Oh yeah…Craig made nine bucks an hour before that job. During his tenure, he averaged over $80 an hour—all because of a thing called "work."

- ## E Is for Enjoy

  Learn to have fun when you are with your clients. It may be your job, but this is also your life. You want to look back on it with great stories and fond memories. Ditch the stress, and allow yourself to enjoy what you can about your day.

• R Is for Responsibility

You are 100% responsible for your life. Not 80%, not 50%, but 100%! Only you can determine whether you succeed or not. Nothing guarantees your success, not even all the training available in the world on non-confrontational sales. Without taking responsibility for your life, you are left allowing life to throw you around and destroy you. Taking responsibility for everything at all times puts you back in the driver's seat.

Experience is what you make of it. If you decide to be responsible for everything in your life, good things will happen to you every single day.

Why Not the Best?

What is keeping you from being the best?

You can be the greatest non-confrontational seller the world has ever seen!

All you have to do is commit yourself to the art of improvement. I read an autobiography by President Jimmy Carter called *Why Not Be the Best?* In it, Jimmy explains the title of his book. He told of when he had applied for a nuclear submarine program and was called in for an interview with Admiral Rickover. Here is his statement:

I had applied for the nuclear submarine program, and Admiral Rickover was interviewing me for the job. It was the first time I met Admiral Rickover, and we sat in a large room by ourselves for more than two hours, and he let me choose any subjects I wished to discuss. Very carefully, I chose those about which I knew most at the time—current events, seamanship, music, literature, naval tactics, electronics, gunnery—and he began to ask me a series of questions of increasing difficulty. In each instance, he soon proved that I knew relatively little about the subject I had chosen. He always looked right into my eyes, and he never smiled. I was saturated with cold sweat.

Finally, he asked a question and I thought I could redeem myself. He said, "How did you stand in your class at the Naval Academy?" Since I had completed my sophomore year at Georgia Tech before entering Annapolis as a plebe, I had done very well, and I swelled my chest with pride and answered, "Sir, I stood fifty-ninth in a class of 820!"

I sat back to wait for the congratulations which never came. Instead, the question: "Did you do your best?"

I started to say, "Yes, sir," but I remembered who this was and recalled several of the many times at the Academy when I could have learned more about our allies, our enemies, weapons, strategy, and so forth. I was just human. I finally gulped and said, "No, sir, I didn't always do my best."

He looked at me for a long time, and then turned his chair around to end the interview. He asked one final question, which I have never been able to forget—or to answer. He said, "Why not?" I sat there for a while, shaken, and then slowly left the room.

This is a story I share with my team members to illustrate how easy it is to go through life at any number less than 100%. How often do you do your best? When was the last time you had a perfect day of effort and persistence? I want you to ask yourself...

...*Are you doing your best?*

The answer, unfortunately, is usually no. And there is never a viable and justified response for that answer. There is no excuse for not doing your best. Ever.

How Clover Leafing Works

Clover leafing is a useful strategy for drumming up new leads while working on a sale or after you have just closed one. While you are on site, you have the unique opportunity to talk to all the neighbors to see if they would like your service.

It is an excellent practice to go knocking on the three to five doors to the left of the home you are working with, the three to five homes to the right of the home you are working with, and the five to seven homes directly across the street once you are done with your closed sale. You will need to create a script that will inspire these neighbors to consider setting a meeting with you to discuss how your product could benefit them as well. There is no better time to name drop, create credibility, and get new leads and sales than after you are hot off the last sale.

The clover leafing represents the leads and sales you can get simply by being on location and having a prepared script and then hitting the left, center, and right (like the shape of a three-leaf clover). Scripting is key here.

Dan's simplified Clover Leafing Script might go like this:

Dan: *Hi there, I have a couple of quick questions for the owner of the home. Is that you by chance?*

Customer: *Yes, that's me.*

Dan: *Oh great, I'm sure you know the Johnson family just across the way? They were fortunate enough to qualify for our new program. My job is pretty easy out here. We help homes in this neighborhood qualify for a unique program that helps homeowners like you take advantage of XYZ so that they can _____. I just have some basic questions to see if your home might qualify.*

Continue on to regular script.

Success and Consistency

What does success mean to you?

A lot of people do not even consider the answer to this question. Success is a journey. A good definition might be that success is the progressive realization of a worthy ideal. You can be a man pumping gas at the corner station and be a huge success if that is what you had predetermined and decided to master. It is different for everyone.

Success in non-confrontational sales means:

- Getting people to listen when you speak and keeping them highly engaged.
- Closing more sales on a regular basis by truly helping people and providing a valuable service.
- Solidifying your sales to not have a higher-than-expected cancellation rate and ensuring people understand your offering.
- Using non-confrontational sales practice in all relationships—even those outside of work—to create dynamic communication that deepens and enhances already meaningful relationships.

In all my years of sales, one thing predicts success more than any other: consistency! It is the name of the game. You have to show up and work hard every day, every week—no matter what.

Chapter 12

RESOURCES & EXERCISES

"Setting goals is the first step in turning the invisible into the visible."
TONY ROBBINS

Congratulations! You now have the tools you need to become a formidable, non-confrontational direct seller. All that remains is for you to take the first steps into practicing this incredible high performance selling method.

This means you need some resources and exercises to sharpen your skills. In this chapter, you will find some motivating pieces of advice along with the resources and exercises you need to become a world class direct seller—without that horrible push factor.

Employee Motivation & Rewards

One of the best ways to stay motivated is by setting up a weekly and monthly goal tracker that is connected to either a personal rewards system or rewards within the company.

Commit to doing all things in your power to reach these goals (set them first) and to never give up on finding your way to the end result/reward.

15 WEEK GOAL TRACKER							
Week	Date (fill in below)	15 Week Goal	% Towards Goal	% I Should Be At	Difference (+/-)	On Pace (y/n)	Corrections Needed
Week 1							
Week 2							
Week 3							
Week 4							
Week 5							
Week 6							
Week 7							
Week 8							
Week 9							
Week 10							
Week 11							
Week 12							
Week 13							
Week 14							
Week 15							

The Competition

Competition in your office is necessary to drive your team all the way to the top. I want to give you a challenge that you can replicate whenever you need to boost competitive sentiment. The fact is that the more healthy competition your team has with each other, the more desire they will feel to get out there, make calls, and knock on doors.

Once you have reviewed your team's goals and have recognized the members that have achieved them, you should ask your team about some of the coolest moments that they have had in their lives.

Ask them sincerely, "When was the time that you felt on top of your game for something?"

Most answers will center around when an individual succeeded at something and were named the best, or one of the best, at it. Pure competition drove them to the top, and when they won, it felt like the best thing in the world.

To ignite your team's competitive spirit, have one person at a time raise their hand and openly challenge another person in the room for that day. Bet small things—a hamburger, a drink, the right to be called the champ—or throw something better into the mix.

Let everyone challenge each other one at a time, and write a list on the board. Make sure that everyone is paired with someone and that it is a real competition. Play the game with them, work hard, and they will respect you for it.

Use the chart below as an example:

Team Pairings:

Challenger	Challenged

CONCLUSION

Confrontational sales methods are dead. That is okay. You have learned every tangible technique needed to transform yourself into a non-confrontational direct selling master. At this point, there is nothing you cannot do. You have discovered how to face a human being and to create engagement by being non-confrontational so you can close the sale.

You see, it was never about forcing the client to buy something they do not need and certainly do not want. It was always about the way you thought about yourself and how you instituted the sales methods that you learned during your life.

Now that you have dipped your toes into the waters of non-confrontational sales, I hope you have found new ways to close sales that were previously way out of reach. No more guilt. No more sleaze. Just honest selling, done the right way for people that need your help.

Remember what you have learned and how everything you say either debits or credits your client's emotional bank account. Once they reach that sweet spot, it is up to you to linguistically and charismatically take them all the way to the dotted line.

This is the next generation of sales. This is what will pull you out of that slump and turn you into a confident, top selling master in your sales team. Do not just take my word for it. Practice these techniques for a few days, and drop me a thank you note sometime.

Direct sales has changed. There is a better way, and it has your name on it. I have helped thousands of people discover the magic of non-confrontational sales theory so that sellers will never have to feel like an imposition on their customers ever again. It is time to be the best. No excuses.

Get out there and do it!

Babe Kilgore

REFERENCES

Chapter 1

Quotes About Direct Selling, http://www.goodreads.com/quotes/tag/direct-selling

Doomed For Failure: Hard Selling Is Dead, http://www.financialcopilot.com/doomed-for-failure-hard-selling-is-dead/

Chapter 2

The Greatest Inspirational Sales Quotes, http://www.greatest-inspirational-quotes.com/inspirational-sales-quotes.html

Free Will, https://en.wikipedia.org/wiki/Free_will

Determination, https://en.wikipedia.org/wiki/Determinism

Alexander, Ruth, *Which Is The World's Biggest Employer?* http://www.bbc.com/news/magazine-17429786

Chapter 3

Communication Quotes, http://www.brainyquote.com/quotes/

topics/topic_communication.html

What Are Thoughts Made Of? http://engineering.mit.*edu*/ask/what-are-thoughts-made

Chapter 4

Sales Quotes, http://www.brainyquote.com/quotes/keywords/sales.html

Cherry, Kendra, *Types Of Nonverbal Communication,* http://psychology.about.com/od/nonverbalcommunication/a/nonverbaltypes.htm

Body Language, http://www.slideshare.net/melodeepop/38-gestures-of-body-language

Mirroring – How We Build Rapport, http://westsidetoastmasters.com/resources/book_of_body_language/chap12.html

Schulz, Jodi, *Eye Contact: Don't Make These Mistakes,* http://msue.anr.msu.edu/news/eye_contact_dont_make_these_mistakes

Guide To Reading Microexpressions, http://www.scienceofpeople.com/2013/09/guide-reading-microexpressions/

Chapter 5

Communication Quotes, http://www.brainyquote.com/quotes/topics/topic_communication.html

Reiman, Tonya, *Human Voice – Part II Tone,* http://www.bodylanguageuniversity.com/public/206.cfm

Communications, Textbooks, Boundless Communications, Delivering The Speech, Effective Vocal Delivery, Volume, https://www.boundless.com/communications/textbooks/boundless-communications-textbook/delivering-the-speech-12/effective-vocal-delivery-64/volume-253-4174/

Dlugan, Andrew, *Speech Pauses: 12 Techniques To Speak Volumes With*

Your Silence, http://sixminutes.dlugan.com/pause-speech/

Chapter 6

Phone Quotes, http://www.brainyquote.com/quotes/keywords/phones.html

10 Tips For Call Center Etiquette Excellence, http://blog.talkdesk.com/10-tips-for-call-center-etiquette-excellence

Tung, Jennifer, *The 10 Big Rules Of Small Talk,* http://www.realsimple.com/work-life/work-life-etiquette/manners/10-big-rules-small-talk

Chapter 7

Snider, Emma, *50 Motivational Quotes To Ignite Your Sales Drive In 2015,* http://blog.hubspot.com/sales/motivational-quotes-sales-drive-2015

Thompson, Bob, *Customer Experience Vs. Customer Engagement – A Distinction Without A Difference?* http://customerthink.com/customer-experience-vs-customer-engagement-a-distinction-without-a-difference/

Qualifying, http://www.businessdictionary.com/definition/qualifying.html

O'Brien, Allison, *Competitive Nature And Endorphins: How Do They Effect Us?* http://www.examiner.com/article/competitive-nature-and-endorphins-how-do-they-effect-us

Fleener, Doug, *Successfully Using Assumptive Language,* http://customerthink.com/successfully_using_assumptive_language/

Basu, Rintu, *NLP Persuasion Skills And Preframes Curry Adventures Pt 3,* http://www.thenlpcompany.com/case-study/nlp-persuasion-skills-and-preframes/

Freese, Thomas, A, *The Secrets Of Question Based Selling,* http://www.johnbesaw.com/Secrets_of_Question_Based_Selling.pdf

Polanski, Tom, *Dr. Robert Cialdini And 6 Principles Of Persuasion,* http://www.influenceatwork.com/wp-content/uploads/2012/02/E_Brand_principles.pdf

Chapter 8

Snider, Emma, *50 Motivational Quotes To Ignite Your Sales Drive In 2015,* http://blog.hubspot.com/sales/motivational-quotes-sales-drive-2015

Chapter 9

CPSA's Top 50 Sales Quotes To Inspire Your Sales Team, http://www.cpsa.com/knowledgecentre/SRCArticleRead.aspx?articleID-656

Always Be Closing – ABC, http://www.investopedia.com/terms/a/always-be-closing.asp

Sandilands, Tracey, *Sales Techniques & Closing Scripts,* http://smallbusiness.chron.com/sales-techniques-closing-scripts-24097.html

Sales Closing Tips, http://changingminds.org/disciplines/sales/closing/closing_tips.htm

Hill, Jennifer, *Fund Managers Admit Their Biggest Mistakes,* http://citywire.co.uk/money/fund-managers-admit-their-biggest-mistakes/a799147

Garrett, Chris, *The Persuasive Power Of Specificity,* http://www.copyblogger.com/specificity-in-copywriting/

Chapter 10

Goals Quotes, http://www.brainyquote.com/quotes/keywords/goals.html

Personal Goal Setting, https://www.mindtools.com/page6.html

Getting Back In The Game With Career Goals, http://www.roberthalf.com/officeteam/blog/getting-back-in-the-game-with-career-goals

Montesol, Shana, *Want To Achieve Your Goals? Make Yourself Accountable*, http://developmentcrossroads.com/2011/10/want-to-achieve-your-goals-make-yourself-accountable/

Sisson, Mark, *The Importance Of Non-Negotiable, "No Matter What" Rules*, http://www.marksdailyapple.com/the-importance-of-non-negotiable-no-matter-what-rules/#axzz3ohUO8xll

Martin, Jim, *Kicking Off 3023 With Goals In Life*, https://jimmartinslifeleadership.wordpress.com/2012/01/02/kicking-off-2012-with-goals-in-life/

Priolo, Dario, *7 Essential Ingredients In Creating Effective Sales Training For Sales Teams*, http://blogs.richardson.com/2013/09/06/7-essential-ingredients-creating-effective-sales-training-programs-sales-teams/

Chapter 11

Management Quotes, http://www.brainyquote.com/quotes/keywords/management.html

Konrath, Jill, *If You Think Sales Is A Numbers Game – You're Wrong*, http://www.jillkonrath.com/sales-blog/sales-is-not-a-numbers-game

Servant Leadership, Putting Your Team First, And Yourself Second, https://www.mindtools.com/pages/article/servant-leadership.htm

Mattson, Dave, *4 Tips For Persuading People By Listening To Them*, http://www.entrepreneur.com/article/241678

Lee, Kevan, *The Science Of Motivation: Your Brain On Dopamine*, http://blog.idonethis.com/the-science-of-motivation-your-brain-on-dopamine/

How To Create Desire To Win At Sales, http://www.realbusinessgroup.com.au/how-to-create-desire-to-win-at-sales/

Saltzman, Barry, S, *How To Make Your Workplace Fun, Productive, And Creative*, http://www.fastcompany.com/3044879/hit-the-ground-running/how-to-make-your-workplace-fun-productive-and-creative

The Dangers Of Cynicism, http://www.richsmanagementblog.com/the-dangers-of-cynicism-at-the-office/management-principles/

Chapter 12

Robbins, Tony, http://www.brainyquote.com/quotes/quotes/t/tonyrobbin147791.html

Dean, John, H, *10 Tips To Improve Your Sales Performance,* http://www.sellingpower.com/content/article/?a=10089/10-tips-to-improve-your-sales-performance

Bradberry, Travis, *How Successful People Work Less And Get More Done,* http://www.inc.com/travis-bradberry/how-successful-people-work-less-and-get-more-done.html

Jannarino, Anthony, *5 Ways To Be Optimistic In Sales (Or Anything Else),* http://thesalesblog.com/blog/2010/02/20/5-ways-to-be-optimistic-in-sales-or-anything-else/

Hopkins, Tom, *What Free Throws And Sales Have In Common,* http://www.tomhopkins.com/blog/tag/consistency-in-sales

ABOUT THE AUTHOR

Babe Kilgore has spent his career mastering the psychology of direct sales. He has personally trained over 10,000 direct sales representatives through his sales and recruiting training mastery programs. Babe has taken multiple sales companies to the top of their industries in multiple arenas. Babe attended BYU for his academic training, but his formal education came from personally knocking on tens of thousands of doors selling products door to door and recruiting thousands of dynamic individuals and teaching them the art of sales. Babe is highly respected for his integrity and ethics in direct sales, and he lives by the motto that sales techniques are skills—therefore *anyone* can learn to sell and even master it.

Made in the USA
San Bernardino, CA
07 July 2017